EDICATION

The Holy Spirit

In this the year dedicated by the Catholic Church to the Holy Spirit, it is to this friend whom I do not want to live without that I dedicate this narrative.

My Three Mothers

I dedicate this book also to motherhood throughout the universe - to my Heavenly Mother, the Blessed Virgin Mary; to my earthly mother Andrea Morin; and to my wife Regina, the mother of my two beautiful children. Without their influence and love it would have been impossible to write this story. I love them immeasurably.

In thanksgiving to God for the grace in allowing me to write this conversion story, I echo the words of St. Therese of Lisieux:

At the close of my life's day I shall appear before thee with empty hands, for I ask not Lord, that Thou would count my works...All our justice is tarnished in Thy sight.

Table of Contents

Acknowledgements

I cannot adequately express my gratitude to the people who have dedicated much of their time fostering the apostolate of Respond Ministry. To Sister Mary Lucy Astuto, Dorothy Green, Peggy Mitchell and Ann Bonnano my sincere thanks for all your support. My special gratitude to Respond Ministry's coordinator, Char Weaver, for her tireless efforts in keeping Respond Ministry organized and running on a daily basis.

A heartfelt thank you also to the countless friends who have supported Respond Ministry and the *To The World* music throughout the years. You are too numerous to name but you know who you are. You have my endless gratitude. May God bless you richly.

Special thanks to those who selflessly gave their time to edit this book: Joseph Cortese III, Annie Ogilvie, Rick and Jennifer Condon, Bill Kuhn, Char Weaver, Mary Harper, Mary Sue Eck, Robert and Deb Rowald, Jerry and Margherita Green and Regina Morin.

Your contribution has been immeasurably valuable.

Introduction

Regardless of how far we have strayed from our faith, all of heaven rejoices when even one lost sheep comes back to the fold. This is the story of one who strayed, but was given the grace to not only return to the fold, but become God's servant as well.

Evidence over the centuries supports the existence of the powerful relationship between the Blessed Virgin Mary and the Holy Spirit. Throughout history, Mary's numerous visits remind us of the importance of living the Gospel. Mysteriously, God and Our Lady are calling many back to the fold, especially in Medjugorje, where for years Mary has continued giving daily and monthly messages. Her mantle of motherly love can evaporate even the greatest of obstacles separating us from communion with her Son, Jesus. In a loving and motherly way she beckons us to be reconciled with God and man. Through this personal conversion to God through Jesus, the Holy Spirit mystifyingly allows us a glimpse of Mary's intercessory role in the faith. We then are able to join with her and the Holy Spirit in an unquestionable knowledge that Jesus is Lord and that, yes, God exists.

For several years I have experienced the promptings to write this book. I have waited until this appointed time because confirmation, courage, and love, which come only from God and His Holy Spirit, were needed to complete such a task.

We live in a time of great mercy and grace. Hearts continue to be transformed and the Holy Spirit is being poured out in great measure.

I will pour out my spirit upon all flesh. Your sons and daughters shall prophesy, your old men shall dream dreams, your young men shall see visions. Even upon the servants and handmaids, in those days, I will pour out my Spirit. (Acts 2. 16-18, Joel 3. 1-2)

This powerful Holy Spirit is here for the asking and everyone has potential access to Him. The ability to hear Him, perhaps, is just a matter of tilling the soil of our hearts and to be open and allow Him to plant the seeds of grace.

If you love me, you will keep my commandments. And I will ask the Father, and He will give you another advocate to be with you always, the Spirit of Truth, which the world cannot accept, because it neither sees nor knows it. But you know it, because it remains with you, and will be in you. I will not leave you orphans. I will come to you. (John. 14: 15-18)

As you read this book I hope you will recognize a certain calling to your heart; maybe not to write or sing music, but to respond to God's and Our Lady's call with the qualities, gifts, talents and charisms unique to your own life. The simplest deed done in love indicates to others that you are a child of God and a recipient of His grace.

What follows is a witness to a personal calling that to this day mystifies me. Although beyond my human understanding, time has confirmed what I believe was directed to me; that I be an instrument, a servant for the Holy Trinity and Our Lady in writing, singing and performing music they have given me. Although I am human and unworthy, they have granted me the courage and the love to act on their behalf.

I believe God calls each one of us to a role in His great plan for the salvation of mankind. Through many happy and sad events in my life, God has been merciful and Our Lady continues to call.

JANUARY 25, 1987: *Dear children, behold, also today I want to call you to start living a new life as of today. Dear children, I want you to comprehend that God has chosen each one of you, in order to use you in a great plan for the salvation of mankind. You are not able to comprehend how great your role is in God's design. Therefore, dear children, pray so that in prayer you may be able to comprehend what God's plan is in your regard. I am with you in order that you may be able to bring it about in all its fullness. Thank you for having responded to my call.*

The Blessed Virgin Mary at Medjugorje

Grace

Grace has five effects on us: first, our soul is healed; second, we will good; third, we work effectively for it; fourth, we persevere; fifth, we break through to glory.

St. Thomas Aquinas

CHAPTER 1

Where there is no obedience, there is no virtue; where there is no virtue, there is no goodness, no love; and where there is no love there is no God: without God we do not go to Paradise.

Servant of God, Padre Pio

AN AWAKENING

The 7th of January, 1988, was a bitterly cold night in Des Moines, Iowa. My bedroom, located on the east side of the house, was often very cold. Some extremely cold nights I would go to the much warmer living room and sleep on the couch. It was about 11:00 p.m. when I went to sleep in my living room that night. I was awakened abruptly and found myself gazing at the ceiling, listening to three words, "HEALING, DIRECTION, PURPOSE." The voice was that of my mother, Andrea Morin. Immediately, I looked toward her favorite straight-back chair and glanced at the small alarm clock on the end table. It was 3:00 a.m. I sat up on the couch and wondered what I had just heard. Of course my mother wasn't there. She was thirteen hundred miles away at her home in Fitchburg, Massachusetts. So, what were these three words spoken in her voice? Not more than thirty seconds passed when the same three words were repeated; "HEALING, DIRECTION, PUR-

1

POSE." The words again sounded like my mother's voice just as if she was sitting next to me on the couch. Now I was fully awake. The chills chased up and down my spine and tears welled in my eyes. My first reaction was fear. "What is going on here?" I asked myself. The fear was quickly replaced with a tremendous feeling of love and comfort. I had the sensation of someone actually holding me. My next thought was to call my mother to see if anything was wrong. I quickly dismissed that idea. If anything had been wrong with my mother, my brother certainly would have called me. Besides, how could I ever explain this to my mother without causing her to worry. She wouldn't sleep for weeks if I told her something this unbelievable.

Suddenly, I was prompted to get a pad of paper and a pencil. I quickly walked the few feet to my desk. On returning to the couch, I found my mind saying, seemingly independent of my will, "I am listening." Then I began to write the following: "JERRY, MY SON, YOU NEED TO BE HEALED OF MANY THINGS IN YOUR LIFE; THINGS THAT HAVE AFFECTED YOU ALL OF YOUR LIFE; THINGS THAT ORIGINATE EVEN FROM PAST GENERA-TIONS." I was in awe as the words continued. Could this be the Holy Spirit? Could this be my deceased father? "WE WISH FOR YOU TO BE HEALED. WE WILL LEAD YOU TO WHERE THIS HEALING WILL TAKE PLACE, BUT YOU MUST FOLLOW AND OBEY. OUT OF THIS HEAL-ING WILL COME NEW DIRECTION AND PURPOSE. IT WILL BE WHAT WE HAVE PLANNED FOR YOUR LIFE." I stayed in the listening posture with pencil in hand, but the speaking had ended. My body was able to relax from its heightened state. For the next hour I read and re-read the writing trying to comprehend its meaning. Sleep escaped me the rest of the night. I felt as though I had been plugged into high voltage electricity. Through the night I remembered a similar experience during Holy Week in 1983. The intensity was the same. The message was again presented

2

to me in a manner that seemed inscribed into my very soul; so clear, so concise, so pronounced. I knew this was not a song. The words were instructions; comforting and reassuring, but "heavy".

The next morning I went to work as usual but was very tired. I couldn't forget the three words and the accompanying explanation heard earlier that morning. I felt prompted to call my mother in Massachusetts. I began to reflect on the strong faith of my mother and felt an intense need to call her.

As a young boy, I watched my mother's prayers help our family through the difficult times, especially when my father was ill and unable to be gainfully employed. I believe her prayers were all we had to rely on. My older brother became the sole supporter for the family during much of my young life, so faith and trust in God was instilled at an early age, especially throughout those difficult times. My mother's life could be best characterized as one of constant prayer and total dependence on God. She did her very best to instill upon her three children that God does answer prayer.

By mid-day the curiosity of hearing my mother's voice compelled me to call her. I knew I must approach the issue delicately. In the conversation I asked her if she was praying for anything in particular for me. I was hoping her response would be "healing, direction and purpose." Instead she replied, "No. I just pray for you from the time I get up in the morning to the time I go to sleep at night. You're always on my mind. I just want to see your life settled and at peace." I knew I had disappointed her over the years as she watched the different paths my life took. I decided it would not be wise to share what I had just heard in my living room. We said our good-byes and I hung up the phone.

Out of obligation as a Catholic, I had been going to Mass on Saturday evening or early Sunday morning. I also attended a non-denominational church where I sang with their choir every Sunday morning. I knew the pastor very well and felt my singing with them was fine as long as I carried out my Catholic duties. I especially enjoyed the wonderful music selections and majestic sound. I decided I should share my living room experience with that Protestant pastor. He was a very good man who had respected me for my commitment to the choir and to my Catholic faith. He listened attentively and seemed very interested. He advised me that this was something between God and me and that I needed to simply trust in God's leading.

And the leading did continue. I could actually sense myself coming closer to something that would be important for my life. The voice of wisdom and instruction was getting clearer and would be heard at the most peculiar times. It was in the month of May when I shared the January happening with a friend. When she heard about my experience, her eyes widened. She immediately asked if I had heard about a village in Eastern Europe where some children were seeing The Blessed Virgin Mary. As I shook my head, she said my living room experience reminded her of an article she had just read. She told me she would send me the information if she could find it. This was of little interest to me at the time. I was too consumed in seeking what I felt was very close to revealing itself. If God was truly trying to help me get my life in order, then I wanted this also. It was time to allow God, whom I believed knew me better than I knew myself, to lead the way to my wholeness. I was trusting in Him completely. I wanted this rightness more than ever. I figured at my age, being single and childless, it was time to find out what God wanted of me.

CHAPTER 2

If you ever want to know the real qualities of a man...judge him by his attitude to his mother.
If you want to know the quality of a religion, judge it exactly the same way, that is, by the attitude that it bears to the Mother of Our Blessed Lord.

Bishop Fulton J. Sheen

A MOTHER'S GIFT

Tue to my friend's promise, by late May I received a package in the mail. I opened it, scanned the enclosed article about the Blessed Virgin Mary appearing to several young children and tossed the packet on my dining room table. Two weeks later, while attending to unpaid bills, I felt an urge to reopen the package. This time I was compelled to read the information thoroughly. It contained a photocopied article about a small, rocky, mountain village in Yugoslavia (now Bosnia) called Medjugorje (pronounced Medjuh-goriah). The one-page article explained that the mother of Jesus was appearing to six young children and giving messages to them that pertained to their lives, the village and the future of the world. She called herself the Queen of Peace, the Most Blessed Virgin Mary. Her first appearance was June 24, 1981, the Catholic feast day of

St. John the Baptist.

Initially, I read with skepticism. However, as I read the messages of Mary reportedly conveyed to the young children, my attention quickened. Something very strange began to happen. While reading Mary's messages, I began hearing Holy Scripture echo inside my mind. This happened more clearly with each message I read. I came to a place in the article where she quoted a particular passage to the children as a most important Scripture (Matthew. 6: 24-32). My eyes widened. I knew its meaning immediately, because a few years earlier I had received a song through the Holy Spirit entitled "I'm In Love" which had this same passage as its basis. Immediately a chill came over my entire being and tears filled my eyes. Through this internal hearing of Scripture and confirmation of my song, I sensed the Holy Spirit was confirming to me these Marian messages were from God. Was Mary a messenger sent by God to this modern world? I immediately opened my Bible to Matthew, Chapter 6 and I also pulled out the song "I'm In Love." The sensation was one of absolute awe. What was going on here? To what is this all leading? Was this all just a coincidence?

No one can serve two masters. Either he will hate the one and love the other, or he will be devoted to the one and despise the other. You cannot serve both God and mammon. Therefore I tell you, do not worry about your life, what you will eat or drink; or about your body, what you will wear. Is not life more than food and the body more than clothing? Look at the birds of the sky; they do not sow or reap, they gather nothing into barns, yet your heavenly Father feeds them. Are not you more important than they? Can any of you by worrying add a single moment to your life span? Why are you anxious about clothes? Learn from the way the wild flowers grow. They do not work or spin. But I tell you that not even Solomon in all his splendor was clothed like one of them. If God so clothes the grass of the field, which grows today and is thrown into the oven tomorrow, will he not much more provide for you, O you of little faith? So do not worry and say, "What are we to eat? Or what are we to drink? Or what are we to wear? All these things the pagans seek. Your heavenly Father knows that you need them all. (Matthew. 6: 24-32)

I'm In Love
(To The World I)

I'm in love, I'm in love
I'm in love and my heart is where it ought to be
I'm in love, I'm in love
I'm in love with a friend whose loving me
I'm in love with a friend who cared so much for me
That He died so that I might find the way
I'm in love and I've found His Spirit's set me free
And it's getting clearer every day
I'm in love, I'm in love
I'm in love and my heart is where it ought to be
I'm in love, I'm in love
I'm in love with a friend whose loving me

I don't worry about the clothes I wear
Or food I'm gonna eat
Take a look at the flowers in the field
King Solomon, even with his wealth he never had
Clothes as beautiful as one of these

I'm in love, I'm in love
I'm in love and my heart is where it ought to be

I'm in love, I'm in love
I'm in love with a friend whose loving me

And I hope that when you hear
This love song that you see
That this love's the light of Jesus Christ in me

Upon finishing the article, an incredible feeling came over me of being engulfed in love. This was the same sensation I experienced earlier on the 7th of January when I heard the voice in my living room. I was perplexed yet my heart felt such warmth and a sense of the Spirit of Truth. I believed God might actually be confirming to me through Scripture that this event with Mary and the children was true. But why was I being reminded so clearly of my January experience?

I have much more to tell you, but you cannot bear it now. But when he comes, the Spirit of truth, he will guide you to all truth. He will not speak on his own, but he will speak what he hears, and will declare to you the things that are coming. He will glorify me, because he will take from what is mine and declare it to you. Everything that the Father has is mine; for this reason I told you that he will take from what is mine and declare it to you. (John. 16: 12-15)

The awareness associated with reading the copied article never escaped me after that night. Even at work I could hear Mary's messages echoing in my mind. This continued for approximately a month until I was overcome with an indescribable urge to go to Medjugorje. The article mentioned that although Yugoslavia was part of the communist block countries, pilgrims had recently been permitted to travel there and were coming from all over the world. For weeks, every time the thought of journeying to this village entered my mind, I felt a tremendous surge of peace and joy in my heart. I had never previously heard anyone mention this obscure event or place and the pull to learn more was very great.

Several attempts to find additional information yielded nothing. Finally, while on a company business trip, I found a small Catholic bookstore that had recently received a new book written by Father Svetozar Kraljevic, <u>In The Company of Mary</u>. I eagerly read the book and became convinced that something truly remarkable was happening in that village. It brought to mind many stories I had heard at Immaculate Conception Grade School and later at Notre Dame High School in Fitchburg, Massachusetts. The sisters had told us about Mary's visits to such places as Lourdes, France and Fatima, Portugal. Up until I was eighteen I wanted to be a priest. Remembering these stories about Mary brought all those tender thoughts back home to me.

Here I was at the threshold of an event that could be one of the most profound events of our time if it was true. Was this a sign of our times? Had we reached a critical point in our history that God would need to send Mary the mother of Jesus, to warn us to change our ways? Could this possibly be the wisdom of God to send this humble woman, who brought Jesus here two thousand years ago, to prepare the world for His return? Could this be just a hoax? My curiosity increased with every unanswered question.

By the time the month of July arrived, I had made a couple of phone calls to travel companies. Finally I located an agency in Chicago that was beginning to plan trips to this village. I quietly investigated what the trip entailed and told the agent I would call her back if further interested. In the meantime, I felt I must be careful not to discuss this with too many people. I wasn't quite ready to tarnish my high-flying, independent bachelor persona. I also took particular care to protect my professional image. They certainly would not want to know about this at my place of work. No, this was between God and me.

In early August, 1988, perhaps more out of curiosity than anything, I made the final decision to visit this mysterious village. I called the travel agent and arranged for the trip. A few days later in the quiet of my living room, I heard the soft inner voice whisper to me; "I WANT YOU TO TAKE YOUR MOTHER WITH YOU" I remember protesting out loud, but the voice continued, "YOUR MOTHER IS SEVENTY NINE YEARS OF AGE. YOU MAY NOT HAVE MUCH MORE TIME LEFT WITH HER ON THIS EARTH. WOULDN'T THIS BE A GREAT GIFT TO GIVE TO YOUR MOTHER?" It suddenly occurred to me that perhaps this was what God was calling me to do. Was I being asked to fulfill something for my mother while we still had time together on earth? After a couple of days pondering and praying, I began to feel good about this possibility. Perhaps this trip explained why my mother's voice was heard in my living room. Maybe this was a time that God wanted for my mother and me to share together. Why else would the whispering voice tell me to take her? However, this posed a problem; telling my mother I wanted to take her to Yugoslavia, a communist country, seemed an impossible task. However, it occurred to me if God truly was bringing all of these encounters and experiences, and if He really did want my mother to go on this journey, then she would somehow say yes. In actuality, I knew it would take a small miracle to get her to agree to accompany me.

The more I pondered the possibility that God was somehow mysteriously directing me to take my mother to this village, the more anxious I became to ask her to go.

I remember clearly the morning I called her and asked her if she would like to go on a vacation with me soon. Immediately she asked where I had in mind. I paused and asked her where she would like to go. With excitement in her voice, she said one of her favorite places was the shrine of St. Anne-de-Beaupre, in Quebec City, Canada. Oddly enough, this was a special shrine to the mother of Mary, St. Anne. I found this response to be very interesting. At least she had a shrine in mind. Then I said, "Actually, I would like to take you to Yugoslavia." There was silence. "Where?" she said; "Yugoslavia," I answered. "Where is that? Isn't that over the ocean? How many hours trip would that be? Why would you want to take me there?" she asked. Then she went on to give every reason why she would be unable to make this kind of trip. "You know I have high blood pressure. My nose bleeds on long trips. I probably would be required to have a physical. I'd have to check with my doctor to see if I could go." Then, before I could respond, she said, "It seems to me I just read something about Yugoslavia this week." "Oh, what was that?" I asked. She said, "Something about some **children seeing the Blessed Virgin Mary**. I believe it was in the Readers Digest." I was shocked. Chills came over me again. "That's it!", I nearly shouted. She paused for about ten to fifteen seconds and then responded, "It's telling me I should go." This was a phrase I had heard her say all my life growing up, "It's telling me..." I now recognized "It" was the Holy Spirit.

I told her I would make all the arrangements. When I hung up the phone I was in awe of the conversation. Whatever was happening seemed to be increasing in intensity. I felt wonderful. My heart was jubilant. Maybe I could finally do something special for my mother. I could give her this gift of bringing her to a place where the Blessed Virgin was possibly appearing. I thought she deserved this trip and I was overjoyed to provide this experience for her. I knew my mother had a deep devotion to Mary. She always prayed the Rosary. I didn't know anyone who had such deep faith in God and prayed the Rosary so often. I could vividly see her in my mind's eye reverently holding her rosary every morning before I went to school. I felt happy for my mother and concluded that it was for her that all of these coincidences and mysterious experiences were happening to me. It was comforting to have some explanation for the mysticism of the last eight months. I was thanking God for orchestrating these events for my mother. The excitement and sense of mystery was unmistakable in anticipation of taking this pilgrimage with her.

The trip was scheduled for mid-November, 1988. The next couple of months were spent quietly preparing, acquiring visas and passports, and waiting anxiously for the morning when I would leave from Des Moines, Iowa, to go to Boston, Massachusetts where I would join my mother. During this time of preparation, my living room once again became the site of another strange encounter.

One of my friends with whom I shared my travel plans asked if I had ever seen the movie called *The Song of Bernadette*. He thought I could find it at a video store, as it was an Oscar winning movie from 1943. I located it, took it home, and quietly watched it in my living room. Amazingly, the experience of watching this resulted in the same chilling feeling I had experienced before. After the movie was over, I sat back in the recliner and turned off the lights. Within minutes I saw internally what appeared to be just some clouds. Out of the clouds a figure came toward me. I thought, "Is my mind playing tricks?" The lady seemed to be about twenty-five yards away from me. To her left and behind her were two very large shiny steel doors that opened toward me from the middle. The doors were partially opened. She raised her left arm, pointed and looked at the doors then looked at me. With her arm still stretched upward she would look at the doors for about five seconds and then look at me. This happened three times. Then I heard the woman say, "BE-HIND THESE DOORS IS MY SON. FOR MANY YEARS YOU WOULD TRY TO GET THESE DOORS TO MY SON OPENED BY YOURSELF." Immediately I knew what she meant. "YOU WOULD TRY SO HARD. YOU WOULD GET THE DOORS PARTIALLY OPEN AND THEY WOULD SLAM SHUT. MY ENEMY WOULD NOT ALLOW YOU TO OPEN THEM FULLY. I AM GOING TO LEAD YOU TO WHERE THESE DOORS WILL NEVER CLOSE AGAIN. I AM GOING TO LEAD YOU TO **WHERE I WILL MELT THEM FROM EXISTENCE.**"

The experience was overwhelming. When it was over I was sitting in my chair with tears streaming down my face. These words would remain etched forever in my mind, in my very soul. Although I could not understand why, I was beginning to be convinced something profound was happening in my life. Why was I experiencing Mary? Was her motherly comfort what I needed to heal the wounds of the past? I was trusting that God would bring an understanding to me in time.

Meanwhile, I continued attending weekly Mass but also sang in the choir at the non-denominational church. Again I confided in that pastor. I shared the story of the small, rocky mountain village and the fact that I would be going to Yugoslavia on a pilgrimage with my mother. Immediately he cautioned me to beware of Satan's tricks, that he disguises himself as an angel of light. I knew this to be a necessary precaution, but after our discussion I realized that the Protestant perspective of Mary was different from the perspective in my Catholic faith. I decided not to make our theological differences an issue. Later that week, the music minister of the same church called me into his office to tell me I should think twice about going to such a place that sounded so demonic. "Visions of Mary are certainly of the devil," he cautioned. I told him I would give him an assessment of the place and the event when I returned. After all, I was doing this for my mother not for myself.

The days passed quickly and soon the time for our trip arrived. I had the tickets and passports and had prepared everything the travel agent requested. There was a reserved excitement running through me, a little fear of the unknown, and a tremendous anticipation of witnessing what many pilgrims to Medjugorje had already witnessed.

CHAPTER 3

There is no sinner in the world, however much he may be at enmity with God, who does not return to Him and recover His grace, if he has recourse to Mary and also her assistance.

St. Brigitta of Sweden

PILGRIMAGE

The morning of November 13th I boarded the plane in Des Moines and headed for Boston. My mother lived in the lower level of my brother's home. This was a house I built for them in 1983. My sister Claudette and my brother Maurice were at the airport to greet me. It was obvious they were concerned about this trip to Yugoslavia. They couldn't quite understand why I would want to take our seventy-nine year-old mother to a communist country. Even more confusing to them was the fact that she wanted to go. I couldn't blame them for not understanding, for I could barely understand it myself. I recall my sister saying, "I suppose if you guys die there, what better way to go than being where the Blessed Virgin is." I assured them everything would be fine.

The next morning my mother and I flew from Boston's Logan Airport to Kennedy Airport in New York. We were to rendezvous with other pilgrims from all parts of the country. Once at our gate, we were introduced to one another by our travel guide. It was interesting to note that each one I conversed with seemed to have this sense of being led or "called" to take the journey. I felt for an instant I was in the Steven Spielberg movie, *"Close Encounters of the Third Kind."* Our tour guide briefed us on the expectations and formalities of entering communist territory. She was successful at making the entire group feel comfortable and unafraid.

Finally, we were airborne. The plane was a huge Yugoslav airbus. There were over two hundred people on board destined for Belgrade, Yugoslavia. I was surprised to see so many others making the same journey. I wondered how all these people found out about this event. Did they also have similar mystical experiences?

My mother was quite comfortable, and the trip, though thirteen hours plus, seemed to go by quickly. I read a book a friend had suggested, Healing The Wounded Spirit, by John and Paula Sanford. My friend directed me to this book after I had shared with her my January living room experience. She was particularly interested in what I had heard about healing from past generations. I was so captivated by the book's message of healing through the power of the Holy Spirit I practically read the entire book before landing in Belgrade, the capital of Yugoslavia. One of the chapters, "Generational Sin," kept me totally absorbed.

When we landed in Belgrade we were transferred to another plane destined for Dubrovnik, an old, historically significant seaport of great beauty. My attention was immediately drawn to the armed soldiers at the baggage claim area.

They were everywhere and soberly watching everyone very closely. They randomly gave some of the travelers a full body and baggage search. I was wearing jeans, a black leather jacket and sun glasses. My mother moved closer to me and whispered; "Did you see how the guards were watching you. They're going to think you're a spy." I assured my mother everything would be all right and not to worry, but it was unnerving.

After successfully meeting the customs requirements, we boarded one of the many buses awaiting our arrival. From Dubrovnik, it would be a three-hour trip up into the mountains to the small village of Medjugorje. About twenty minutes had lapsed when our travel guide asked if we wanted to pray the Rosary. Immediately my mother was ready. I noticed in her hands a pretty rosary of cut glass and silver. She said her sister Stella had given her the rosary several years ago before she died.

Almost everyone in the bus was familiar with the prayers. The last time I remembered praying the Rosary was as a young boy. Despite not having beads of my own, I began to follow and join in. Soon a peace began to settle in my heart. I slowly became reacquainted with the beautiful prayers of all fifteen decades. I could tell my mother was really enjoying this, for praying is the very essence of her life. I had a sense of satisfaction that the trip felt so right for us.

We arrived in Medjugorje very late in the evening and were immediately grouped into local homes where we would spend the rest of the week. It was common for the homeowners to accommodate the pilgrims during their stay. They even seemed to look forward to meeting us and dining with us. Before departing for the evening, our guide instructed us on our intended schedule for the week. As I lay in bed that night I remembered many details in Father

Kraljevic's book. Reality was setting in that this was no longer a distant event. We were really here to witness it first hand.

The First Day

After an enjoyable breakfast and getting to know our host family, we attended the English-speaking Mass at St. James, the parish church. Holy Mass is what my mother lived for. It was a wonderful experience for both of us. I couldn't remember ever seeing so many people in one church during a Mass.

April 3, 1986: *Dear children, ... Therefore, consciously live the Holy Mass and let your coming to it be a joyful one. Come to it with love and make the Mass your own. Thank you for having responded to my call.*
The Blessed Virgin Mary at Medjugorje

The church was absolutely packed and the faithful were standing everywhere. The overflow crowd poured out into the courtyard to listen to the Mass over the loud speaker. There were approximately twenty priests up on the altar concelebrating the Mass. It was beautiful. People were extremely reverent throughout the Mass. Rosaries could be seen everywhere in the hands of young and old alike.

June 12, 1986: *Dear children! Today I call you to begin to pray the Rosary with a living faith. That way I will be able to help you... That way you shall understand the reason I am with you this long. I desire to teach you to pray. Thank you for having responded to my call.*
The Blessed Virgin Mary at Medjugorje

There seemed to be a joy, a peace here that I had not felt at any other Mass in my entire life. It didn't take long to realize we were participating in an event that had reached all

18

corners of the world. The principal celebrant, who was from Ireland, gave a homily that centered on the message of Medjugorje and the importance of Our Lady's visits there.

During the Mass, an American Franciscan priest, Father Philip Pavich, gave us special instructions and an historical perspective of this event. He informed us that two of the six visionaries, Ivanka Ivankovic and Mirjana Dragicevic no longer received daily apparitions, but that Mary would appear to them at special times and on certain feast days. The other four visionaries, Ivan Dragecivic, Marija Pavlovic, Jakov Colo and Vicka Ivankovic saw her every day. I could sense the responsibility that this priest had in ensuring that the pilgrims maintained a sense of piety and order throughout their visit. Mass was celebrated every hour in a different language for pilgrims of that particular tongue. When we stood in the courtyard of St. James Church we would hear conversations all around us in a variety of different languages. The international effect of Medjugorje was obvious.

After Mass, I noticed long lines of people out on the grounds of the church and wondered why so many people would want to eat lunch that early. I looked closer and was amazed to find that these were lines for the Sacrament of Reconciliation. Priests were scattered intermittently, throughout the church grounds, hearing confessions in German, Italian, English, Dutch, Spanish, and many other languages. My mother and I both remarked that we had never seen confession lines like that.

June 6, 1985: *Dear children, During these days people from all nations will be coming into the parish. And now I am calling you to love: love first of all your own household members, and then you will be able to accept and love all who are coming. Thank you for having responded* *to my call.*

The Blessed Virgin Mary at Medjugorje

Later that evening our guide instructed us to return to St. James Church where the Rosary would be prayed and Our Lady would appear. At this time, the four young adults were receiving their daily apparitions in the choir loft. Again, the church was tightly crowded and many pilgrims poured out into the courtyard. This time, however, the Rosary was prayed in Croatian, the native language. It was amazing to witness the local residents during the Rosary. They would kneel on the hard marble floor the entire hour. Their display of reverence and holiness brought tears to my eyes. I had never seen such piety. Singing was also part of the Rosary and the church was filled with every voice joyously raised in song. A complete silence came over the church when the Rosary ended. This was the time of Mary's visit to the young visionaries in the choir loft. The apparition lasted about ten minutes then the praying and singing resumed. Finally, we were dismissed.

My mother and I walked back to the guest home to gather for supper. On the way back she commented that she had never experienced anything like that. She was especially impressed with the faith of the local residents. We overheard pilgrims discussing their experiences. Several people at the dinner table spoke about seeing certain phenomena during the time of the apparition, including colored lights. One lady then remarked that she witnessed the white host inside the Monstrance, in which the Blessed Sacrament was exposed, turn a brilliant blood red. Others said they saw the face of Jesus inside the Tabernacle, while others described flashes of light during the time of the apparition. I remained at the table after dinner and thought, "Here we go, here come the crazies and fanatics." I didn't see anything unusual or notice anything strange that night except the tremendous faith of the people, especially of the local parishioners. That was phenomenal to me. We retired for the night and there was a wonderful sense of peace within me. Others could experience weird things if that was what they needed. I had already experienced my share of weird things before getting here.

The Second Day

The second full day followed somewhat the same schedule. In the evening, after the Rosary and apparition, we heard personal stories that seemed to defy logic. At that point I wondered if Satan was working, but if so, why were so many in our group moved toward the Sacrament of Reconciliation? I didn't think that was what Satan wanted. At dinner again many shared their personal experiences and were overcome with joy.

August 29, 1985: *Dear children, I am calling you to prayer! Especially since Satan wishes to take advantage of the yield of your vineyards. Pray that Satan does not succeed in his plan. Thank you for having responded to my call.*

The Blessed Virgin Mary at Medjugorje

Others at the table were very quiet and reserved and wondered what to make of the place. I was one of those, but as long as my mother was enjoying herself, I was happy. We retired for the night. Again, a wonderful sense of peace prevailed. Back home in Des Moines life had been too hectic to feel this kind of peace.

The Third Day

Early that morning I was awakened by the delightful sound of a rooster. While still in bed, I was staring up at the ceiling listening attentively to music. The music wasn't from outside. It seemed like it was from inside and outside of me at the same time. It was a beautiful, majestic song with glorious instrumentals. I had never heard this song before. The peace in my heart while listening was unlike anything I had ever felt before. I lay there quietly and listened intently for several minutes. I got up and while in the shower began hearing the words and began singing the song. There came the Holy Spirit chills again! Although the shower was cold water, this was a different kind of chill; the same kind I had experienced many times before.

Everyone met for breakfast in the dining room and began to prepare for the morning Mass. Several had heard me singing in the shower and commented how beautiful the song was.

The Lady of Medjugorje
(Title Song - *To The World I*)

O the lady is calling
Is calling us all
When you hear it, will you follow
Follow the call?
Her graces are flowing
Her beauty aglow.
She's a lady of splendor
A lady to know

Now the lady is calling
Is calling us near
Come closer, she is shining
She asks not to fear
Her light is a brilliance
Transcends all the earth

22

Now all come together
Come all now to her

To the mountains, Medjugorje
Lady of Peace
You're blessed, O Mary
It's love that you bring
Our hearts will not wonder
Why she has come
She's here on behalf of His only Son

O the lady is truly
A light for our lives
A beacon in darkness
For all hearts and minds
And if you hear her calling
To please let Him in
Hear the lady, she's calling again

To the world, she is calling
To please let Him in
For the lady, blessed lady
For the lady will not come again

Peace. Peace. Peace.

This third day would turn out to be one that would change my life forever. It was on this day and the next that many unexplained mysteries would unfold.

My mother and I again attended the morning Mass. Afterward, we were walking across the church courtyard when my mother suddenly stopped and gasped, "Look at the sun!" At first I thought she was having some sort of dizzy spell. She repeated, "Look at the sun." I glanced up and suddenly I was staring into an almost noonday sun, on a perfectly clear day, and yet, the sun looked like a pearl. It began to shimmer, spin, and generate a spectrum of colors - gold, yellow, red, green - over and over again. Suddenly, the sun began to pulsate. My mother and I described the changes to one another as they occurred. This lasted for about ten minutes with many others watching too. I'm not sure how to explain the sensation other than sheer awe. What was happening? What did it mean? The experience certainly affected both of us. My mother turned to me and said, "I really believe Mary is appearing here." A person standing next to us, sharing in this experience, explained how this had been a sign of the Blessed Virgin's presence in the apparitions of Fatima, Portugal in 1917. Later, at a small bookstore, I found a book on Fatima and read what had taken place at the last apparition on October 13, 1917. Approximately seventy thousand people were present to witness the "miracle of the sun." I was amazed at the similarities to what we had just witnessed.

Approximately an hour after seeing this spectacle with the sun, I experienced an indescribable desire to go to confession. There was a joy springing up from my very soul at just the thought of confession. This was definitely a new sensation for me. I waited in the English speaking line and finally entered the confessional when it was my turn. I was sitting face to face with a Franciscan priest. I immediately noticed the peace and radiance on his face. He asked my name and I told him, "Jerry." No priest had ever asked my name in confession. He told me he was a visiting missionary priest from Africa. I noticed his gentle eyes and kind demeanor. He seemed to radiate joy with his constant smile. It had been over seven years since I had been to confession, so he patiently helped me get started. I was truly surprised to recollect past sins that I never thought I would remember. A tremendous weight was lifted from me as I felt cleansed of old baggage.

After receiving absolution for my sins, I thanked the priest and left. When I closed the door of the confessional, I instantly heard within me; *Unless you become like a little child you cannot enter the kingdom of heaven.* I knew this passage of Scripture, but why was I hearing this now? Immediately a deep understanding came to me and this passage took on new meaning. What I had just completed by receiving the Sacrament of Reconciliation made me a little boy again in my heart. Was this God's way of telling me I was forgiven? The wellspring of joy within me was unmistakable.

Little by little, Jerry Morin, straight-faced guy in a black leather jacket and sunglasses began smiling and feeling wonderful. I never remembered feeling this way before. No. Wait! I could remember feeling this way as a young boy. In grade school confessions were taken seriously. The Catholic sisters took us to confession as a class at least once a month. Is this why Our Lady stressed to the visionaries the importance of going to confession monthly? I realized confession had removed the darkness from my being, from my very soul. The relevance of this being an important sacrament was now a special and personal experience. In my heart I was once again the boy of my youth. When I joined my group later we were all like kids, joyfully sharing the experiences of the day.

That afternoon our tour guide led us to hear Marija Pavlovic, one of the visionaries. While Marija was speaking, the sun went through its gyrations again, and everyone there noticed it. Many were pointing again in amazement. This lasted for about ten minutes. But I was still cautious not to allow myself to be deceived. I would analyze everything from my quiet, reserved perspective just waiting to convince myself, somehow, this was all a sham.

That afternoon I began thinking about my father, who had passed away in 1970. He had been a professional musician. I began thinking of how music had also been a major part of my life. Fifteen years earlier I had been a professional singer and performer. I spent approximately six years on the road singing in some of the finest dinner clubs throughout the United States, Canada, the Bahamas, Bermuda and Puerto Rico. I traveled thousands of miles during those years. Ultimately, the life-style led to heartache and disappointment, almost to the point of destroying my very soul. When I left the music business I never wanted anything to do with music again. My mother, however, constantly reminded me of the gifts God had given me. She always wished for me to use my musical ability for God or somehow for the Church. Now, suddenly, I awaken with a song I had never heard before! As I was receiving the words to the song, it occurred to me that this was a song about Our Lady. In fact, the words were helping me to better understand the occurrences in Medjugorje. God was revealing something to me about this place through that music. I thought, "How mysterious!" I had an eerie sense of this being something very special, but I did not understand it.

That evening we again attended the Rosary in preparation for Mary's visit to the visionaries. At 6:00 p.m. the Rosary began. Again the church was full and hundreds more were out in the courtyard. A very kind gentleman noticed my mother and me standing and offered her his place in the pew. I remained in the back of the church alone. I was praying the Rosary fervently along with everyone. The young visionaries were in the choir loft above me. Then exactly at the time of the apparitions, I experienced something I will never forget. The sensation was like leaving my body and having my spirit transported to some other place. My best attempt at describing this event was a state of total rapture. While in this

26

state, I listened to the following words being spoken to me: "COME SING MY SONGS TO ME, COME SING MY SONGS FOR ME. PREPARE THE SONG." Then, as if someone were asking the question for me, I heard, *"WHERE IS THIS?"* The voice replied, "YOU ARE IN MY THRONE ROOM OF GRACE." This dialogue seemed independent of my control. The voice then said, "THE SONG WILL BE HEARD THROUGHOUT THE WORLD, EVEN IN DIFFERENT LANGUAGES " Again a question was asked for me. *"HOW CAN THIS BE?"* The voice replied "WE WILL GRANT YOU THE COURAGE TO DO THIS. DO NOT FEAR. WHEN COMPLETED, RETURN AND PLACE IT BEFORE MY FEET TO BE ANNOINTED AND BLESSED BEFORE IT GOES OUT TO THE WORLD." When this ended and I regained awareness of my surroundings, I found myself standing in the back of the church absolutely spellbound and in tears. Quickly I wiped my face and looked around to see if anyone had noticed me. It took awhile to assimilate what I had heard, but I knew these words would remain forever in my mind, in my heart and in my very soul.

Stunned, I walked out of the church and found my mother. I told her I had just been spoken to in the church. She asked, "What did *it* say?" I conveyed to her everything I heard. She looked at me and replied, **"Why don't you do whatever He tells you to do!"** I was startled by her response. Immediately I identified the words my mother said to me as being the same words Mary spoke to the servants at the wedding feast at Cana. Again tears filled my eyes. I felt as though the Blessed Virgin Mary had just spoken to me through my mother. This was almost too much for me to handle!

I was struggling for composure as we made our way to the home where we were staying for supper. I was still trying to assimilate and make rational sense of what I had heard in the church. The scene played over and over in my mind and I fought to keep the tears from falling onto my plate. COME SING MY SONGS TO ME. Who was asking me to sing and what songs are they talking about? What did this mean? What was I to do, and how was I to accomplish what was asked of me? The voice had said, "WE WILL GIVE YOU THE COUR-AGE..." What did that mean? What kind of responsibility would this bring? What was so special about this particular song? More unanswered questions. So many emotions! I pondered all of this through the night, until, exhausted, I finally fell asleep.

The Fourth Day

I was again awakened by the sound of the rooster. Immediately, I remembered the voice and the instructions COME SING MY SONGS TO ME. Was there another song to be heard? I had been awake probably only thirty seconds when I heard the soft gentle voice again; "COME TO THE MOUNTAIN, COME TO THE CROSS." I recognized the voice and didn't hesitate. I dressed quickly and quietly left the house. It was very early in the morning and still dark as I started walking in the direction of Mt. Krizevac. Within about fifteen minutes I reached the base of the mountain. Some in my group had already made the steep climb earlier in the week, but I had not attempted it. I wondered why I had heard "come to the mountain , come to the cross" on this particular morning.

Our Lady had told the visionaries to pray from the heart. I began ascending the mountain and prayed the Rosary as I climbed. This was the beginning of a deep level of prayer for me. I was filled with an indescribable joy and love for God. As I prayed I was reflecting on my confession of the day before. The voice and instructions echoed through my mind. Daylight was approaching and love was surrounding me. Like a wellspring, I could feel this tremendous warmth rising and bubbling within me.

I climbed for about forty-five minutes before finally arriving at the top of the mountain. In awe, I gazed up at the huge cement cross that majestically crowned the highest point. This was my first glimpse at seeing the massive thirteen-ton cross. While gazing at the huge structure, I was reminded of the courage and perseverance of the local parishioners who constructed it in 1933 in commemoration of the 1900-year anniversary of Christ's crucifixion. Suddenly, I noticed a person standing at the base of the cross. It looked like a man. The person's back was turned toward me and a hood covered his head. We were the only two people on the mountain. As I was studying the figure I heard the soft voice instruct me: "ASK FOR HANDS TO BE PLACED ON YOUR HEAD." At this point I seriously began to question what I was hearing. Was my imagination playing tricks on me? What does this mean now? I don't know this person. He will think I'm crazy. As I reflected on how everything seemed to be happening with some kind of mystical direction, I gathered my courage and slowly approached the large cross.

My knees were weak, for I was hesitant to convey to this person what I had just heard. I stopped at the base of the stairs leading up to the cross. The man stood one step higher and still had his back to me. I cleared my throat and he turned around and looked into my eyes. Immediately I fell to my knees, holding my chest in sheer disbelief. I found myself looking into the eyes of the priest who had heard my confession the day before. **"Jerry, we meet again,"** he said in his deep voice. How did he remember my name? How could he have possibly remembered me from all the confessions he heard yesterday? Hesitatingly and stunned I asked, "Father, can I tell you something? I heard something said to me just before I came up these stairs." "What did you hear?" he asked. "I am to ask you to place your hands on my head." As

I remained kneeling, his reply overwhelmed me. "Jerry, I noticed you coming up the mountain at that lower bend. As I watched you **I heard the very same directions.**" He then placed his hands on my head and began to pray. My body started to tremble. I began crying uncontrollably. In that instant something very powerful took place. I experienced something leave me from the very depth of my being. I was free. This was a spiritual healing beyond anything I had ever experienced.

It took a few moments to regain my composure as the priest and I visited. At my request he gave me his name and address in Malawi, Africa. I hugged him and told him how grateful I was for this special "divine appointment". The priest then left me alone on the mountain. In those few moments his obedience to God was to be instrumental in changing my life forever.

The sun was beginning to rise over the distant mountains. The day was perfectly clear and it was magnificently beautiful from on top of the mountain. I was so grateful to God for this morning's experience. I knew something had taken place beyond my comprehension; something very powerful; very special. As I gazed out over the majestic scenery, I was seeing with what seemed to be new eyes. The sun was rising on the horizon and this scene would always be etched in my mind.

I went over to a small patch of boulders to sit and reflect on the happenings of that morning. I kept thinking of how I had come here for my mother. Why were all of these things happening to me? Then I heard these words, "DO YOU REMEMBER THE VOICE YOU HEARD IN YOUR LIVING ROOM LAST JANUARY? THAT WAS NOT THE VOICE OF YOUR EARTHLY MOTHER. THAT WAS THE VOICE OF YOUR HEAVENLY MOTHER. AND, NOW THINK, WHERE DID SHE LEAD YOU? HALF WAY AROUND THE

WORLD TO COME TO THE FOOT OF THE CROSS OF HER SON JESUS CHRIST, WHERE HEALING, DIREC- TION, AND PURPOSE ARE BEING GIVEN TO YOU." At that moment I froze. Chills just kept going up and down my spine. In that instant I clearly understood what God was trying to do with my life. It felt as if heaven's doors had opened to me. I was quickly reminded of the lady's words "I WILL MELT THEM FROM EXISTENCE." Was this what Our Lady meant by melting the steel doors between her Son and me? Again, this was almost too much for me to handle! As I gazed out over God's beautiful creation I was reminded of a Scripture passage I had memorized some fifteen years before. (2 Corinthians. 5: 17)

So whoever is in Christ is a new creation; the old things have passed away; behold new things have come. And all this is from God, who has reconciled us to himself through Christ...

I was being given an entirely new start; a new life. My heart was pounding so hard in my chest, I thought it would burst from this infusion of grace. Now I could forgive my- self for personal failures. I could forgive my mother for some of the hurt I carried from boyhood. Forgiveness and love were all around, in and through me. One by one I remem- bered people by whom I had been wronged in the past. With each thought I forgave the hurt. It was as if chains were literally falling off of me. I felt a tidal wave of love envelop me.

What eye has not seen, and ear has not heard, and what has not entered the human heart, what God has prepared for those who love him, this is revealed to us through the Spirit. (1 Corinthians. 2: 8-10)

Throughout my young Catholic life I had been taught

that Mary leads us to Jesus. Never before had I experienced such a profound personal experience with the Blessed Mother. God was showering me with graces. With every passing minute I was hearing one profound statement of wisdom after another about my life; Mary; the Holy Spirit; the events of Medjugorje and my mother. Other thoughts were directed toward forgiveness. It was as though an infused knowledge about my life's experiences was part of God's plan for my life. My heart was bursting with gratitude to God and Our Lady. It seemed They had worked within me what They promised.

I am confident of this, that the one who began a good work in you will continue to complete it until the day of Christ Jesus. (Philippians. 1:6)

As I sat there reflecting, the voice told me to have confidence that what I was hearing was indeed from above. If I could believe these last few days' experiences were part of the fulfillment of that January 7th encounter, then I could believe with even greater confidence in what was being asked of me in Medjugorje. "WE CALL YOU BACK TO THE FAITH OF YOUR BOYHOOD, NOT FOR WHAT YOU SHOULD EXPECT, BUT RATHER FOR WHAT YOU SHALL NOW GIVE TO IT." Upon hearing this, a sense of courage and intense seriousness seemed to be instilled, yet the joy and peace were unmistakable.

By now others were coming up the mountain. I began to sing "How Great Thou Art" while I descended the rocky terrain. I wanted the whole world to know of God's and Our Lady's love for us. Suddenly, I understood what Our Lady meant in one of her early messages to the young visionaries, *"Be reconciled."* I felt like a new person coming down from the mountain. It made me think of Moses on Mt. Sinai. God had written His instructions to Moses on stone tablets. It felt as though God had just burned His messages into my heart.

I hurried to St. James Church for the 10:00 a.m. Mass. During the liturgy a tremendous sense of sorrow for my sins came over me. I cried throughout the entire Mass. I stayed in the back of the church with my head down hoping no one would notice me. God was washing me through and through. I recognized that what was happening was a total cleansing and purification. (I have learned many times since that tears can be one of God's great gifts for healing.) It was at this time that an inner sense of understanding came regarding the message heard in the church the night before. I felt the message had two distinct parts. I was to prepare the song I heard on the third morning and I felt I was to prepare the songs I had received over the years and somehow begin to sing them.

FEBRUARY 25, 1987: *Dear children,...pray, and in prayer you shall realize a new way of joy. Joy will manifest in your hearts and thus you shall be a joyful witness of that which I and my Son want from each one of you. I am blessing you. Thank you for having responded to my call.*
The Blessed Virgin Mary at Medjugorje

So many questions and mysteries were beginning to be answered. Through the intercession of Mary, the Holy Spirit, and probably my own mother's prayers, I had been led to Medjugorje. Here I could feel the barriers melt away between God and myself. This morning I was more grateful than ever for my mother. I remember at one point wondering how I would ever explain this experience to my mother or to anyone for that matter. It was so deeply personal and unlikely.

The Fifth Day

The remainder of the trip was filled with tremendous graces. I found myself absolutely loving to pray the Rosary. We were able to meet with visionaries Ivan Dragicevic and Vicka Ivankovic. They spoke to us of their experiences with the Blessed Virgin and answered many of our questions. Their responses were reflections of the holiness and gentleness of Mary's daily communication with them.

Our tour guide escorted us by bus to the neighboring small village of Tihaljina. We were privileged to meet Father Jozo Zovko. This was the Franciscan priest who had been imprisoned for sheltering the six young children from the communist soldiers soon after the apparitions first began. He explained to us in a remarkable three-hour talk that he had also had the privilege of seeing Our Lady. During his talk, this holy Franciscan priest invited us to find five small stones at the base of the mountain where Mary first appeared. They were to be carried home and placed on the altar we were encouraged to make. The five stones on our altar were to remind us of the five main messages that Our Lady was giving at Medjugorje: prayer; faith; fasting; conversion and peace. He spoke on the significance of each of these elements. He also recommended we place a Bible on our home altar.

Prayer

August 25, 1989: *Dear children, today I call you to prayer. By means of prayer, little children, you will obtain joy and peace. Through prayer you are richer in the mercy of God. Therefore, little children, let prayer be the light for each one of you. Especially, I call you to pray so that all those who are far from God may be converted. Then our hearts shall be richer because God will rule in the hearts of all men. Therefore, little children, pray, pray,*

pray. Let prayer begin to rule in the whole world. Thank you for having responded to my call.

The Blessed Virgin Mary at Medjugorje

Faith

November 25, 1997: *Dear children, today I invite you to comprehend your Christian vocation. Little children, I led and am leading you through this time of grace, that you may become conscious of your Christian vocation. Holy martyrs died witnessing: I am a Christian and love God over everything. Little children, today also I invite you to rejoice and be joyful Christians, responsible and conscious that God called you in a special way to be joyfully extended hands toward those who do not believe, and that through the example of your life, they may receive faith and love for God. Therefore, pray, pray, pray that your heart may open and be sensitive for the Word of God. Thank you for having responded to my call.*

The Blessed Virgin Mary at Medjugorje

Fasting

September 26, 1985: *Dear children, I thank you for all the prayers. Thank you for all the sacrifices. I wish to tell you, dear children, to renew the messages which I am giving you. Especially live the fast, because by fasting you will achieve and cause me the joy of the whole plan, which God is planning here in Medjugorje, being fulfilled. Thank you for having responded to my call.*

The Blessed Virgin Mary at Medjugorje

Conversion

January 25, 1988: *Dear children, today again I am calling you to complete conversion, which is difficult for those who have not chosen God. I am calling you, dear children, to convert fully to God. God can give you everything that you seek from Him... Therefore, dear children, put your life in God's hands. I bless you all. Thank you for having responded to my call.*

The Blessed Virgin Mary at Medjugorje

Peace

November 29, 1983: *Dear children, I am your good Mother, but Jesus is your great friend. Fear nothing in His presence, but give Him your hearts. From the depth of your heart tell Him your sufferings. In this way, you will be revitalized in prayer, your heart set free, and in peace, without fear.*

The Blessed Virgin Mary at Medjugorje

Father Jozo ended the evening by individually praying over the hundreds of pilgrims present. One after another were "rested in the Spirit" (lying prostrate on the floor), including fellow priests. Father Jozo's presence exuded holiness. When he had completed his talk, a spiritual fire enveloped my heart. What a tremendous gift it was to have received his blessing. It would bring me strength during the days ahead.

Grace

The first work of the grace of the Holy Spirit is *conversion,* effecting justification in accordance with Jesus' proclamation at the beginning of the Gospel: "Repent, for the kingdom of heaven is at hand." Moved by grace, man turns toward God and away from sin, thus accepting forgiveness and righteousness from on high. Justification is not only the remission of sins, but also the sanctification and renewal of the interior man.

Our justification comes from the grace of God. Grace is *favor, the free and undeserved* help that God gives us to respond to his call to become children of God, adoptive sons, partakers of the divine nature and of eternal life.

CHAPTER 4

Since the goodness of God is so great that one single moment suffices to obtain and receive His grace, what assurance can we have that a man who was a sinner yesterday is so today?

St. Francis de Sales

HEADING HOME

On our last day in Medjugorje, the pilgrims in our group prepared for the journey back home. Many of us took the time to purchase some last minute mementos of our pilgrimage. I bought several rosaries and then proceeded to find the five small stones Father Jozo had asked us to have on our home altars. As we began the three-hour bus ride back to Dubrovnik, I already missed the small, peaceful village. I didn't want the peace I was experiencing in my heart to end. My mother shared this melancholy feeling.

On our way to Dubrovnik everyone in the bus began praying the Rosary. I reached for one of the new ones in my backpack and behold! The links, crucifix, and medallion had all turned a gold color. Overwhelmed, I showed it to my mother and asked if I could see her rosary. As she took it out of her purse we both were amazed to see it was similarly gold! This was the same silver rosary, a gift from her deceased sister, which I had admired at the beginning of our trip. Noticeably embedded in the gold of the crucifix were many bright colors, sparkling like gold dust. My mother was visibly moved when she saw the transformed rosary. I was so happy for her because if anyone deserved these graces, she did. It was a clear sign to me that heaven was pleased that we made the journey.

We had a delightful visit in the ancient city of Dubrovnik. On our way home, I finished writing out the words and music to the song I had received on that third morning, "The Lady of Medjugorje." I was beginning to gain the confidence to carry out the instructions heard only a few days earlier in St. James Church...."COME SING MY SONGS TO ME...PREPARE THE SONG." But how would this happen?

It was during the layover in Belgrade, Yugoslavia, that I received another song. I recall sitting on the floor in the airport awaiting instructions from our travel guide. I was pondering and trying to assimilate all of the events of the week. (This assimilation would continue for weeks, months, and even years to come.) Suddenly, almost absent mindedly, I began singing to myself. It was another song I had never heard. I listened intently to every word as I scurried to find any kind of paper and pencil in my backpack. Within the next twenty minutes, "Lovely Lovely Lady" was written.

Lovely, Lovely Lady
(To The World I)

You're a lovely, lovely, lovely, lovely lady
Such a sight for all the world to see
If they do not see, let them still believe
'Cause you are here and that's all right by me
You are here and that's all right by me

You're a lovely, lovely, lovely, lovely lady
So secure when you are holding me
You're love takes me away
Oh I wish you could stay
A little while longer holding me
'Cause where you are is where I want to be

Chorus:
You've opened up my heart like no other
I sometimes can't believe it
when I think about your love
Now I'm seeing all my sisters and my brothers
I think that what they're seeing
that it's you inside of me
You're a lovely, lovely lady what I know you to be
You're a lovely, lovely, lovely, lovely lady

Instrumental
Repeat Chorus:

It's with your love that you will touch the world
Soon the day will come when each and every one
Comes to know you in a special way
They will sing and here is what they'll say
You're a lovely, lovely, lovely, lovely lady
In the heart is where they'll know your name
When their hearts are won, then you'll show your Son

It's for Him that you send out this song
Sing it now, it's time to sing along

You're a lovely, lovely, lovely, lovely lady

chorus: fade

Another memorable event took place on the plane during our return flight to the United States. Someone in our group knew I had received a new song in Medjugorje and asked me to sing it. I hesitated doing so without accompaniment. Then someone else shouted, "Sing the song!" Somewhat embarrassed, I stood up in the plane, closed my eyes, and began singing "The Lady of Medjugorje." When I finished, I opened my eyes and was immediately humbled to see so many listeners in tears. This was the first evidence of the power of the song. Just then, another person yelled from the back of the plane, "I'll see you on Mother Angelica!" "Who is Mother Angelica?" I asked. I had never heard of her. The person in front of me turned around to explain Mother Angelica hosted a Catholic television program. I found this interesting, but I didn't think much about her or her television program until her name mysteriously came up again a few weeks later.

I sat quietly and prayed and read for most of the return flight. My mother was tired, but very joyful. This was a time that God had appointed for us to be together and share what would probably be one of the greatest events in our lives. I pondered Fr. Jozo's talk. He told all of us that it was no mistake to have come to Medjugorje, but part of God's plan.

Reflecting on all of the events that took place during our pilgrimage, I was in awe. I marveled at how God and

Our Lady lead us to reconciliation if we are open to the promptings. In Medjugorje I experienced a powerful healing. It occurred to me on the plane that this could be the fulfillment of the words heard in my living room on January 7th; "JERRY... THINGS THAT ORIGINATE EVEN FROM PAST GENERATIONS." Was this also the generational healing I had read about on the plane at the beginning of the trip?

In my heart I knew I needed to be serving God and Our Lady in some way. I had new life and now I must strive to repay them. I remembered all the instructions heard while in St. James Church. I didn't know how all of this would take place, but I trusted I would come to understand. I believed God and Our Lady would give me the courage to accomplish whatever it was *They* were calling me to do.

While I was contemplating and reviewing every detail of the instructions, it occurred to me that I was being asked to do something in faith. I was convinced that God, Our Lady, or someone else in heaven had orchestrated this entire pilgrimage. Reportedly Our Lady had said to the children, *Blessed are they who do not see and yet believe.* Unlike the visionaries, I did not see anything extraordinary, except the "miracle of the sun." which had been seen by many other pilgrims. However, the overwhelming series of coincidences and personal experiences left no doubt that there were extraordinary graces being showered on me in Medjugorje.

NOVEMBER 25, 1988: *Dear children,... God is offering and giving Himself to you. But He seeks from you that you answer His call in your freedom.... Thank you for having responded to my call.*

The Blessed Virgin Mary at Medjugorje

"Allow me to be your servant if this is what you wish. I only need you to go before me to show me how to accomplish what you ask of me." After praying these words, I slept peacefully for the remainder of the flight.

MAY 25, 1993: *Dear children, today I invite you to open yourselves to God by means of prayer so the Holy Spirit may begin to work miracles in you and through you.... Therefore, my dear little children, Pray! Pray! Pray! And do that which the Holy Spirit inspires you to do. Thank you for having responded to my call.*
The Blessed Virgin Mary at Medjugorje

My brother and sister were at Logan Airport in Boston to greet us. My mother and I immediately showed them our rosaries and began sharing our many experiences. Our excitement was obvious and they were a bit overwhelmed by our account of the trip.

It was not until we were in the car and on our way to Fitchburg that I explained about hearing the music and instructions. Being very musically inclined, Maurice and Claudette were both interested in hearing the song. They listened quietly as I sang "The Lady of Medjugorje." They were moved by the words and melody. I asked if they had ever heard the song before. Maurice is a fine pianist and an avid music collector. His response came as a surprise. "That song has a resemblance to the chord structure of the song, 'Daddy's Little Girl.' There came the chills again. I thought, Mary... Daddy's little girl. Mary...the chosen woman, daughter of the Father, mother of the Son and spouse of the Holy Spirit. Daddy's little girl! His response triggered an intense realization that Mary was in fact God's special vessel. Had God, Himself, given this song to me to sing about His chosen woman? The thought left me in awe.

The next morning back in Fitchburg, at my mother's home, I awoke with yet another song. Internally, I could hear many people singing this hymn to Mary.

Mary, Queen of Peace
(To The World I)

Mary Queen of Peace we pray
Help us. Show us the way
Mary Queen of Peace we pray
It's with our hearts that we say
We love you
We're so happy you've come
We love you
Lead us to Jesus your Son

And we love you
We are your daughters and sons
We love you
Mother to everyone

Here we bring ourselves to you
Mary, teach us to pray
Through your love we know it's true
That's why we feel this way

We love you
We're so happy you've come
We love you
Lead us to Jesus your Son

Through the Spirit you have come

And to the children be seen
Yet to all that do not see
Blessed be those who believe

And we love you
We're so happy you've come
We love you
Lead us to Jesus your Son

We love you
Help us to answer your call
We love you
We know that you love us all

With the strains of "Mary, Queen of Peace" echoing in my mind, I felt enveloped in the comforting peace that was infused in me at Medjugorje. It seemed that "the voice," heard sporadically before, was now magnified many times. Was this the voice of wisdom, of knowledge, of understanding, of holiness? Suddenly, I understood that I had been flooded with the gifts and power of the Holy Spirit. I had experienced these gifts in varying degrees in the past, but nothing compared to what I was currently experiencing. As I prepared to return home to Iowa, I was filled with love for Jesus and the Spirit of the Lord.

I, the Lord, have called you for the victory of justice. I have grasped you by the hand; I formed you, and set you as a covenant of the people, a light for the nations, to open the eyes of the blind, to bring out prisoners from confinement, and from the dungeon, those who live in darkness. (Isaiah. 42: 6-7)

God seemed to know exactly what I needed to experience in order to remove the doubt from my mind. The sense of gratitude was immense in my heart. This over-whelming sense of gratitude resulted in a quiet resignation to simply say, "Yes, I place my life in your hands."

FEBRUARY 25, 1992: *Dear children, ...I am with you and I intercede for you with God, that He protect you; but I need your prayers and your "Yes".... draw close to God so He may protect you and guard you from every evil. Thank you for having responded to my call.*

The Blessed Virgin Mary at Medjugorje

CHAPTER 5

To escape the distress caused by regret for the past or fear about the future, this is the rule to follow: leave the past to the infinite mercy of God, the future to His good providence; give the present wholly to His love by being faithful to His grace.

St. Augustine

FOOTSTEPS TO CONVERSION

B eing home in Fitchburg opened a floodgate of memories. With God's grace and mercy, the haunting memories that had so often plagued my spirit were beginning to be laid to rest. As the pictures of my jagged past tumbled through my mind, I was taken back to those painful years. As my past flashed before me it became clear that only by God's mercy and grace could this conversion of heart have taken place.

In an earlier time in my life I had often wondered what I had done to experience such desolation, such emptiness in my soul. I participated in two decisions earlier in my life that, for many years, I could not wipe out of my mind. As much as I tried to ignore or bury these decisions, the pain persisted. It was easy to rationalize that it was okay to have followed this course. After all, even the government said it was perfectly legal. And who was the church to tell us what decisions we should make? This was a private decision. Besides, the time wasn't right for children yet. Human rationalization, a byproduct of a desensitized conscience, produced decisive actions involving two little human beings. Two little persons whom I would later find out were boys. Yes, I participated in their physical annihilation; their termination. I fell victim to the ultimate deception.

There was a void within me that nothing or no one could fill. My heart and soul had been torn asunder. Part of me felt like I literally lived in hell. In a very short time I felt the ramifications of my decisions and realized the tragedy. The marriage ultimately ended in divorce.

Being single again, I filled my existence with the luxuries of life - nightlife, sports cars, women and pleasure. I finally reached the lifestyle I believed was right for me. As a successful real estate broker, I had property, money, great-looking cars and women were no problem. I lived in a fifty-two hundred square foot mansion and had no responsibilities to family. I could come and go as I pleased. Yes, I was the picture of success, or so everyone thought. As long as I was busy and on the run I never had to stop to think about how old the two little ones might be. I wouldn't let myself think of it. And if there was a God, the only one I was experiencing was a God who haunted me and condemned me for what I felt were irreparable decisions. I knew I would have to live with my actions for the rest of my life, but perhaps time would eventually allow my mind to forget. For now, I had resolved that a bachelor's life was best for me.

The most difficult times, however, were at holidays or any special times of the year that I could remember as a young boy. Every Christmas was like a recurring nightmare.

I knew I would never see my children open presents; no Santa Claus to talk about; no costumes for Halloween; no Easter Bunny. There would be no one saying excitedly when I got home from work, "Hi, Daddy!" There would be no birthday parties to decorate the house for. There would be no baseball or basketball games to attend, as my father had attended for me. The total effect of this emptiness haunted me to such a degree that I believed I would never allow myself to enter a marriage relationship again.

Then in a mysterious way, I began to realize something had to change. I felt my soul on the edge of a great abyss. In my silent plea to God, mysteriously, the gift of song was granted to me. Through this gift God slowly began to reveal His mercy. Having been a professional musician many years earlier, music was a medium for Him to slowly lead me through this desert to new life. Even the wretched creature I was, God showed His great mercy to me and mysteriously began to enter my life. He began to show me who He was, and that He loved me in spite of myself.

In May, 1981, a friend in whom I had always confided called me one evening to ask if I would like to attend a Catholic conference. He had been a good friend and good business associate. His suggestions always seemed to have a positive impact on my life so I agreed to go. Soon we were headed to Notre Dame University in South Bend, Indiana.

The only two presenters I remember at that conference were Fathers John Bertolucci and Michael Scanlan, T.O.R. These two charismatic priests asked the congregation, which numbered approximately three thousand, to pray aloud the Prayer of Repentance (Psalm 51).

Have mercy on me, O God, in your goodness; in the

greatness of your compassion wipe out my offense. Thoroughly wash me from my guilt and of my sin cleanse me. For I acknowledge my offense, and my sin is before me always: Against you only have I sinned, and done what is evil in your sight-That you may be justified in your sentence, vindicated when you condemn. Indeed, in guilt was I born and in sin my mother conceived me; Behold, you are pleased with sincerity of heart, and in my inmost being you teach me wisdom. Cleanse me of sin with hyssop, that I may be purified; Wash me, and I shall be whiter than snow. Let me hear the sounds of joy and gladness; the bones you have crushed shall rejoice. Turn away your face from my sins, and blot out my guilt. A clean heart create for me, O God, and a steadfast spirit renew within me. Cast me not out from your presence, and your Holy Spirit take not from me. Give me back the joy of your salvation, and a willing spirit sustain within me. I will teach transgressors your ways and sinners shall return to you. Free me from blood guilt, O God, my saving God; then my tongue shall revel in your justice. O Lord, open my lips, and my mouth shall proclaim your praise. For you are not pleased with sacrifices; should I offer a holocaust, you would not accept it. My sacrifice, O God, is a contrite spirit; a heart contrite and humbled, O God, you will not spurn. Be bountiful, O Lord, to Zion in your kindness by rebuilding the walls of Jerusalem. Then shall you be pleased with due sacrifices, burnt offerings, and holocausts; then shall they offer up bullocks on your altar.

Immediately upon praying this I felt a fire in my heart. (Someone later told me it was the fire of purification.) The priests instructed us to gather in small groups of three. Each of us was asked to place our hands on the heads of the other two people. Then, each individual was requested to sincerely ask God for all of the fruits of the Holy Spirit. Each person was invited to ask and pray for three specific gifts of the Holy Spirit to be activated and manifested in their lives. I remember these moments so clearly. We were cautioned to expect to receive what we prayed for. Father Bertolucci and Father Scanlan recited the list of the fruits and the gifts of the Holy Spirit and described the meaning for each.

In Chapter 5 of Ephesians we see *the fruits of the spirit are love, joy, peace, patience, kindness, generosity, faithfulness, gentleness and self-control.*

In Chapter 12 of 1 Corinthians the gifts of the Spirit are explained: *There are different kinds of spiritual gifts but the same Spirit; there are different forms of service but the same Lord; there are different workings but the same God who produces all of them in everyone. To each manifestation of the Spirit is given for some benefit. To one is given through the expression of the Spirit of Wisdom; to another faith by the same Spirit; to another gifts of healing by the One Spirit; to another mighty deeds; to another prophecy, to another discernment of spirits; to another varieties of tongues, to another interpretation of tongues. But the one and the same Spirit produces all of these, distributing them individually to each person as he wishes.*

The three gifts I asked for that evening were wisdom, mighty deeds, and prophecy. We were then encouraged to partake in private confession. It had been probably ten years or more since I had experienced the Sacrament of Reconciliation. Did I even want to mention the tragic decisions of my past? I managed to gain the courage to confess even these experiences. The priest was extremely patient with me and very sympathetic. With that confession I felt the beginning of an inner transformation. Peace began to surround my heart. I felt grace for the first time in a long while. Hope and a spiritual conversion had begun in my life. I believe it was while attending that conference that the Holy Spirit began His renewal work in me.

For the next couple of years I experienced a pervasive thirst for Holy Scripture and a soulful hunger for God. Also in those years, I began developing a relationship of prayer with the Holy Spirit and I was being led to understand that He was here to help guide and comfort me. I learned He was available to me, indeed to anyone, twenty-four hours a day, any place I would find myself. In these times of communication I experienced great joy and peace.

One of the first songs I ever received was a result of this communication developing with my God. The lyrics I received seemed reflective of this newfound personal relationship with Yahweh, Jehovah, Abba Father, the Alpha and Omega, the King of Kings, Lord of Lords, the Shepherd and the Lamb that was slain. Other songs soon followed. Accompanying almost all lyrics was what seemed to be a natural melody. This was the very private Jerry Morin, resolved in the belief that these written songs were simply a quiet and private extension of love and communication with my God, content in the belief these songs were only for me and for my spirituality.

Just You and I
(To The World I)

Antiphon:
Heavenly Father we praise Your name
Till the day You come back to reign
We lift Your name higher than stars in the sky

Heavenly Father it's just You and I.

Yahweh the name above others
Abba the Father we praise
You're King of Kings and Lord of Lords
When I call You, I trust in Your name

Yes, I call You the Shepherd
Jehovah is also Your name
You're Alpha and Omega, there is nothing greater
You're also the Lamb that was slain

Antiphon:

Grant me Your peace for this moment
This time I'll spend just with You
Take this heart and hear this prayer
And Lord now let me hear You

Lord let Your word come and find me
And draw me closer each day
For I on my own cannot do it alone
With You it's a much simpler way

Antiphon:

Yes my life's forever with You until I die
Heavenly Father it's just You and I.

To sit quietly and hear words and music was like being in an ocean of peace. As a real estate broker why was I hearing these songs? I didn't feel worthy to be writing this kind of music. This was very mysterious to me and yet it was a reality separate from the ways of the world. What intrigued me most was the sense of tremendous peace that accompanied each song.

The difficulty soon came in trying to balance the hectic everyday tangible world with this marvelous communication with the Holy Spirit. Often I longed for the quiet time to pray, read Holy Scripture and just listen. I began to understand the battle every Christian must face. I became acutely aware of the spiritual battle Saint Paul describes:

Finally, draw your strength from the Lord and from his mighty power. Put on the armor of God so that you may be able to stand firm against the tactics of the devil. For our struggle is not with flesh and blood but with the principalities, with the powers, with the world rulers of this present darkness, with the evil spirits in the heavens. Therefore, put on the armor of God, that you may be able to resist on the evil day and, having done everything, to hold your ground. So stand fast with your loins girded in truth, clothed with righteousness as a breastplate, and your feet shod in readiness for the gospel of peace. In all circumstances, hold faith as a shield, to quench all the flaming arrows of the evil one. And take the helmet of salvation and the sword of the Spirit, which is the word of God. (Ephesians. 6: 10-17)

This was a powerful and key scripture in understanding what was needed to remain protected as a believer. I quickly realized that each of the described elements of protection was essential, and the enemy knew how to penetrate the slightest weakness in this fortification. I would be forced to comprehend and to choose on which side of the battle to fight. Many times I found myself in a prayer of consecration to Jesus or to the Holy Spirit.

In Holy Week, 1982, I experienced something that had never happened to me before. While driving my car I was enveloped in peace. Words and music began running in my head as I saw myself standing under the left out-stretched arm of Jesus while on the cross. His head was hanging down to the side and looking directly at me. The blood dripping from his pierced hand nailed to the cross was falling on my head and was completely covering me. The experience and accompanying song had a profound effect on me.

COME TO ME
(To The World III)

Nail your sins upon my cross
Let my blood fall down on you
In My name I'll cleanse you deep inside
Your fears and worries all will flee
They have no hold on you
There is no room for them when you're in Me.

Come to Me when you're in pain
I rescue from the world
The power you'll receive is in My name
By the cleansing of your sins
Your new life will begin
Come to Me and I will make the change

Chorus
Come to Me in My name
Come to Me Jesus Christ
Come to Me and I will give you life abundantly
Come to Me in My name
Come to Me Jesus Christ
Come to Me I want to set you free

I'll be your beacon in the night
Your ship will follow in the light
My words your guide if you will only follow me
My Son the Christ has died for you
Will you give your life for Him too?
Come to Me I want to set you free

Chorus

In my weakness I will walk
And in my courage I will talk
Of Christ the King whose blood is flowing over me
And I will never be the same
Already He has made the change
I trust in Him. Jesus is His name

Chorus

Then, in Spring of 1983, I received what did not appear
to be a song but a set of instructions or directions. In a
mystical encounter with what I believe to be the Holy Trinity, I became aware of the presence of God in a most personal, powerful and dramatic way. These words were privately held for many years, but because they have been and
are still being fulfilled, their importance contributes in the
mystery of this witness. I have constantly been reminded of
this still vivid experience. The sensation was like that of a
hand physically reaching into my chest and wrenching my
heart. This single episode left me bewildered for many
months. As I pondered the words that were spoken to me
that evening, I recognized that much of what was written
were words yet to be fulfilled.

Holy Week, 1983

YOU ARE BEING RENEWED BY MY HANDS.
YOU ARE BEING RENEWED BY MY HEART.
YOU WILL NO LONGER BE THE SAME PERSON.
YOU WILL BE ORDERED AND DIRECTED,
AND THEY WILL BE FROM MY HOME.
THE TASTE I HAVE GIVEN YOU IS A REMINDER OF
　　MY PRESENCE.
THE TASTE WILL REASSURE YOU OF THE
　　TIMES I COME TO YOU.
THIS IS THE POWER OF WHICH I WAS SPEAKING.
IT IS MY RESURRECTION POWER, THROUGH
　　WHICH YOU WILL OVERCOME ALL THINGS IN
　　MY NAME.

YOU WILL NOT HAVE TO WONDER WHAT PEOPLE
　　THINK.
YOU WILL NOT EVEN WONDER WHAT TO SAY.
I WILL PREPARE YOU WITH WORDS OF POWER.

WHAT I HAVE JUST PLACED IN YOU IS ONLY THE
　　BEGINNING OF MY RESURRECTION POWER.
I WILL PLACE IN YOU ONLY AS YOU ARE READY
　　TO USE.
FOR IN MY NAME ONLY CAN THIS POWER BE
　　USED.

I WILL LEAD YOU TO SITUATIONS IN WHICH YOU
　　WILL LEARN HOW TO USE THIS RESURRECTION
　　POWER.
I WILL BRING YOU TO PEOPLE.
YOU MUST PREPARE FOR THEM.

PREPARE YOURSELF WITH MY WORD.

STUDY IT, MEDITATE ON IT; EXHAUST YOURSELF
   IN IT.
FOR THE MORE OF MY WORD YOU HAVE, THE
   MORE OF MY RESURRECTION POWER YOU WILL
   BE GIVEN.
DO YOU NOT UNDERSTAND NOW?

OBEY ME. YOU MUST OBEY ME IF YOU ARE TO
   BE FULFILLED.
I DIRECT ALL ACTIVITY AND YOU MUST OBEY
   ME.

LET NOT EXTERIOR CIRCUMSTANCES BE YOUR
   GUIDE.
BE TUNED TO THE HEART I AM GIVING YOU.
BE TUNED TO THE TASTE I AM GIVING YOU.
IF ONE IS UNSURE, THE OTHER WILL BE THERE.

BLESSED BE ALL THAT YOU TOUCH.
PEOPLE WILL KNOW MERELY BY YOUR
   PRESENCE THAT I AM THERE.

SOON YOU WILL BE COMPLETELY ABSORBED IN
   ME.
I WILL LEAD YOU IN ALL THINGS.
WHEN YOU DO NOT KNOW WHAT TO SAY, I WILL
   COME TO YOU.
I WILL DEFEND YOU AT ALL TIMES.
I WILL COME TO YOU AS MY SON.

GREAT COURAGE, THIS IS WHAT I NEEDED.
TO HAVE YOU IS TO HAVE SOMEONE WHO I
   KNOW WILL CARRY OUT WHAT I TELL HIM.
TO HAVE YOU IS TO HAVE A STRONG ARM FOR
   THE WAR THAT GOES ON AGAINST MY
   KINGDOM.

YOU WILL DELIVER MANY.
YOU WILL SET FREE MANY CAPTIVES WHO ARE

IMPRISONED AND IN CHAINS.
YOU ARE A STRONG ARM AND I WILL USE YOU.
AND YOU WILL CUT LIKE A TWO-EDGED SWORD.
WITHOUT EVEN KNOWING, YOU WILL SET THE
ENEMY UNDER YOUR FEET.

CAN YOU START TO SEE NOW HOW I WILL USE
YOU?
CAN YOU START TO SEE NOW WHY I NEED YOU?
PREPARE...PREPARE.

At first, the experience brought a sense of fear and agitation. Actually, it can be more accurately described as a healthy fear of the Lord. *The fear of the Lord is the beginning of knowledge; wisdom and instruction fools despise* (Proverbs. 1:7). Many questions followed. Why am I experiencing this? What does God want with me? No rational explanation was sufficient. Did I even want to hear this? I would review the words over and over again. Much of the writing appeared to be a revealing of how God was possibly seeing me. Much dealt with my spiritual future and described aspects of my spiritual life yet to unfold. I carried this encounter quietly and reverently, only sharing the discourse with one priest to help me discern and understand better what the words could mean. I was encouraged to simply be open to what God could be trying to show me. I couldn't possibly expect anyone to understand. I couldn't comprehend it myself.

Soon after this encounter, I received the music and words to "You're the Way." I knew immediately the song's basis was the words of Jesus:

Jesus answered, I am the way and the truth and the life. No one comes to the Father except through me. If you really knew me, you would know my Father as well. From now on, you do know him and have seen him: (John. 14:6)

You're the Way
(To The World I)

You have laid down Your life
You gave it to us as a living sacrifice
And You've asked us to follow
Yes we will follow
If we tire You will give us rest
You have given us Your promises
How can we doubt Your promises
When everywhere there's beauty in Your name
You're all the time inside of me
We want O Lord so much to be
The kind of man or woman that You need

Chorus:
You're the way
You're the truth
You're the life
You're the life we breath, You're all we need
Knowing always that You'll understand
You're the way
You're the truth
You're the life
We will follow You our whole life through
And if we fall behind You'll take our hand

We're abiding in Your name
And we hear Your whisper calling like the gentle rain
And Your light's shining brighter

Brighter and brighter
Bringing with it life for us to keep
We are giving You our lives
And we give them to You as a living sacrifice

You go before us in our need
We will follow You will lead
Together we will feed Your sheep

Chorus:

My heart was being transformed with this song and I resolved to try harder to follow Jesus and to allow Him to lead my life. Two days following this experience another grace of music took place. It was about noon, the Wednesday before Easter, 1983, when I stopped at the church to be alone and pray. I had brought with me the written words I had received only a few days earlier. I read the words and, again, I was in awe. I prayed and asked God to help me understand their meaning. I picked up a Bible that was lying in the pew, opened it and read:

I sought the Lord, and he answered me and delivered me from all my fears. Look to him that you may be radiant with joy, and your faces may not blush with shame. When the afflicted man called out, the Lord heard, and from all his distress he saved him. The angel of the Lord encamps around those who fear him, and delivers them. Taste and see how good the Lord is; happy the man who takes refuge in him. (Psalm 34: 5-9)

I was immediately able to relate to David's plea in seeking the Lord. I read the Psalm through once and sat quietly in meditation. Suddenly, I began hearing the psalmist's words in an entirely different fashion. The words came, then the music, then the rhythm. With a sense of urgency, I ran out of the church and hurried back to my home, singing the song the entire way. I didn't want to lose the melody or words. I quickly wrote out and captured the song as it was delivered.

Magnify The Lord (from Psalm 34)
(To The World I)

I sought the Lord, and He answered
He freed me from my fears
My face was changed my life was rearranged
He washed me through my tears

The eyes of Him look on me now
People listen to me
Turn to Him and call His name
All in Him will be free
All in Him will be free

Taste and see the Lord is good
Helpers come from everywhere
His love keeps me in His arms
I look to Him alone
Worship Him in a special way
Sing to Him in a song
For He is faithful to His word
He keeps us free from harm
He keeps us free from harm

Magnify the Lord with me
Let us exalt His name together
Magnify the Lord with me

So you're broken hearted
He's going to make you right
Then you'll magnify the Lord
And come to see His light
And if you turn toward the Son
All the hardness melts away
Your cry will be heard with every word
For the Lord Your God I say
For the Lord Your God I say

Magnify the Lord with me
Let us exalt His name together
Magnify the Lord with me
Let us exalt His name

Every song seemed to be a miracle of grace leaving me with a sense of exhilaration or rapturing. This ineffable grace seemed to function independently of any wish or desire on my part to write anything. One of the determinants seemed to be my willingness to be open to the Holy Spirit's promptings. I not only experienced the songs with my mind, but with my heart and soul. With each song completed I would just put it aside on a shelf. (Some songs took days, weeks, months, or even years to understand in their totality. When the words were fully comprehended, the understanding often came as a surprise to me.) I began to discern certain indications that another song was approaching. One of the indicators was a tremendous enveloping of peace beforehand. Other signs were a noticeable burning of my hands and of my tongue. Every lyric, every song left me wondering why God would gift someone who had been so broken and lost. I still believed they were granted for my own healing and nothing more.

Beginning in 1986, I became engulfed in my professional career working for a large real estate development company. My daily work routine was demanding and led to a lapse in my spiritual life. As I felt myself going the way of the world, I had the constant awareness that I was moving away from God. The songs had stopped also. It seemed the further I moved away from God, the more difficult life became. Old tendencies toward the ways of the world were creeping in. Even though I fulfilled my Catholic duties of weekly Mass, I felt I was gradually losing a very good friend. Emptiness slowly crept into me. Prayer felt senseless and I found myself in conflict.

Realizing this was a negative path, my spiritual resolution for 1988 was to make a personal and concentrated effort to move my life back toward God. I resolved to implement a daily routine of reading Scripture and praying more regularly. I also found joy in singing to instrumental accompaniment tapes in the privacy of my home. New life was springing up within me. I began again to sense the leading of the Holy Spirit in my life. I was regaining my relationship with that long lost friend. It was comforting to know no matter how far away I moved He was always there waiting for me to come back to Him. This was a time of seriously seeking and desiring God in my life, and I was again living the words of David. (Psalm 34) *I sought the Lord and He answered...*

He answered and led me to Medjugorje.

CHAPTER 6

Heaven is filled with converted sinners of all kinds and there is room for more.

St. Joseph Cafasso

A CHANGED MAN

When I returned home to Des Moines after the pilgrimage to Medjugorje, it was immediately clear to me that I was a changed person. I could see that many of the things I thought were important before were actually not a priority at all. Now, having opened a desire to serve God, everything in my old environment seemed different. People and friends even looked different. It was as if I could immediately determine the meaning of situations. Perhaps it was because I saw myself differently. My level of discernment had risen immensely. At first it was a little frightening because I could foresee many of the decisions I would have to make. Simplifying my life became a priority. I was no longer so centered on material things because I recognized that lasting joy and peace come from being close to God.

One of the first decisions I made was to sell the two

Corvettes in my driveway. Only two weeks before I had adored my sports cars. What had once been status symbols had become non-essential baggage. It seemed the only things that were important were the things that would lead me closer to God. Two Corvettes certainly did not meet the criteria. *For where your treasure is, there also will your heart be.* (Matthew. 6: 21)

Also at this time, it became important to make sure my finances were in order. I began to eliminate anything that would be a distraction to living the messages of Medjugorje. I could see how easy it was for people to get into debt and then be consumed with crawling out of it. The Scripture passage Matthew 6:24 took on greater meaning, as I more fully comprehended "possessions." Material things were not the way to the Kingdom of God. I could discern the daily battle of principalities with even greater clarity.

FEBRUARY 25, 1988: *Dear children, today again I am calling you to prayer and complete surrender to God. You know that I love you and am coming here out of love, so I could show you the path of peace and salvation for your souls. ...If you pray, Satan cannot injure you even a little, because you are God's children and He is watching over you. Pray, and let the Rosary always be in your hands as a sign to Satan that you belong to me. Thank you for having responded to my call.*

The Blessed Virgin Mary at Medjugorje
.

Our Lady was being sent as the messenger and the message was clear. Satan was out to destroy human life, minds, hearts and souls. It appeared God was sending Mary with the ingredients to keep our lives protected from these wiles. I could see myself as never before. I could see my past sins and, more importantly, I could see Satan's deceptions and subtle traps. Ephesians 6:10-17 took on new meaning and became a source of strength - *Put on the full armor of God so you will be able to stand firm against the tactics of the devil.*

All of this new understanding and added wisdom seemed to be literally infused into me. I was being healed. My direction would now be different because I was absolutely confident that God, through His Holy Spirit, and with the intercession of Our Lady - and also with the saints and angels - would be leading me along the right path. My direction and purpose here on earth could unfold. The love was unlike anything I had felt in my life. In fact, I questioned if I really even knew love before all of this. I recalled reading the story of how St. Augustine was converted through the prayers of his mother, St. Monica. The realization of the power of a mother's prayers prompted the belief that my own mother's prayers for my life were being answered. Suddenly I understood St. Augustine's words; *"Our hearts are restless until they rest in Thee."*

Only a few days had passed when the overflowing emotion in my heart resulted in another song.

Loving You More And More
(To The World I)

I've been singing a song inside of me
Watching a dream coming true
Every time I get this peaceful feeling
It's when I'm thinking of You

I've been rearranging all my values
No longer wonder what I'm here for

I never get tired of singing
You bring a song for every open door

And when You come through my door at night
It's as wide as it can be
Opening another song to sing
This is what You're bringing to me

Chorus:

The song's I'm loving You more and more
With each day of life You're bringing
The song's I'm loving You more and more
It's You that starts my music playing

I'll keep on loving You more and more
Life's just a word for giving
I'll keep on giving You more and more
With every song that I'm singing.

Whenever I see Your shining face
And feel what You're bringing to me
My mind starts working in rhymes again
Whispering inside of me
Chorus:

The song's I'm......

The days at work went by quickly. Although I worked in a very professional, secular environment, the voice of direction would come to me continually throughout the day. I would go home each night and diligently prepare the songs I was given, especially "The Lady of Medjugorje". I trusted that the Holy Spirit would grant me the courage to do whatever it was that I would be asked to do in the upcoming days and months. I could actually feel the courage building within me. I also had this intense seriousness that I was being called upon to accomplish a mission for them. This tremendous sense of purpose was enveloping me. Why would they need *me* for such a mission? Why would they gift a sinner with such a heavenly song? God could change everything in a millisecond if He wanted and I was beginning to see the wisdom of how God was planning these days. Perhaps Our Lady was helping reveal it to me. Jesus was entrusting the peace of this world to His mother and she needed our help, our prayers, our Rosaries, our special gifts in bringing hearts and minds to God.

JULY 25, 1990: *Dear children, today I invite you to peace. I have come here as the Queen of Peace.... I invite you to become carriers and witnesses of my peace to this unpeaceful world. Let peace rule in the whole world, which is without peace and longs for peace. I bless you with my Motherly blessing. Thank you for having responded to my call.*

The Blessed Virgin Mary at Medjugorje

Reportedly, Mary was giving messages to the visionaries on the 25th of every month to relay to the world. It seemed the bottom line was for Our Lady to reach as many of her children as possible and bring them back to God. With virtually every message from Mary that I read, Scripture would continue to echo in my mind. One message through the young visionaries especially caught my attention. Mary instructed us to place the Bible in a prominent place in the home so we could be reminded to read it regularly. The Bible had always been a source of peace for me. As Father Jozo had suggested, I constructed a little altar in the corner of my bedroom upon which I placed the five stones and my Bible. This became a special place of prayer. There I would find solace from the world by praying the Rosary, reading

69

Holy Scripture and Our Lady's messages and just quietly listening. My heart was set on the path of holiness and it felt so wonderful. This grace of walking toward holiness, of walking toward Jesus, was like finding a lost treasure that I desired with all my heart. If I stumbled, God was merciful and His grace would lead me back on the right path again.

JUNE 25, 1991: *Dear children, ... 'These days while I am with you are days of grace'. I desire to teach you and to help you walk on the path of holiness. ... God will help you discover the true reason for my coming. Therefore, little children, pray and read the Sacred Scriptures so that, through my coming, you may discover the message in Sacred Scripture for you. Thank you for having responded to my call*

The Blessed Virgin Mary at Medjugorje

Many times I was prompted to closely review my writings from 1983. Were these words part of God's plan in preparing me for the work I was about to do? These words, which were once vague and obscure, had come to life with a new understanding. Perhaps God and Our Lady truly had me where they wanted me.

CHAPTER 7

Happy the man whose words issue from the Holy Spirit and not from himself.

St. Anthony of Padua

EMPOWERED

I had been home from Medjugorje a week. That first weekend I decided to go to Mass on Sunday morning and then go sing with the choir at the non-denominational church. Mass that morning was not the jubilant type experienced at Medjugorje. However, I appreciated the Mass much more than I had before my trip. I especially remember the priest's homily. It was like an overview of Our Lady's messages without actually referring to them. As I looked around I could see a lot of blank, mostly passive and restless-looking faces. The piety, the sincerity was not like that of the people attending Mass in the small village of Medjugorje. I saw my own former passivity mirrored in these faces and I found myself much more attentive to the words of the Liturgy. I was awed by the True Presence in the Sacrament of the Eucharist. After receiving the body and blood of Christ I felt an inner glow. I also experienced the same burning sensation as in Medjugorje, as if a flame was ignited inside me. After the final blessing, I hurried to the ominational church to sing.

omething very strange took place at that church that Sunday morning. The choir assembled in front of the congregation like every other Sunday morning. As I looked out, everything looked and felt different. I knew it was different because I was different. I realized I was looking through a new set of eyes and feeling with a new heart. What was I sensing? Jesus was being talked about. The music was wonderful. Suddenly I realized the missing element. Our Lady was not present, nor did she have any importance in this church. I had also experienced the Catholic sacraments with a new depth of meaning. These were missing too. Why did I not see this before? Why was this not important to me before? I had no answers except that it was important to me now, and I felt somewhat out of place.

After the service, the music director asked about my trip. "Did you see anything?" he asked. I shook my head but mentioned I had received some music I felt I was being led to record. He said, "Is it about Mary?" I told him it was but that it was also about Jesus, God the Father and the Holy Spirit. He asked me how many people were visiting Medjugorje. I told him thousands were coming from all over the world - Catholic, Protestant, Muslim, Orthodox, and other denominations. His skepticism was obvious, but I dismissed it and went home.

Not long after that the pastor called me. He said the board members of the church had heard I had taken a trip to Eastern Europe and wanted to know more of the details. The pastor politely asked if there was some way for me to support my experiences with Scripture. I told him I would pray and ask for this to be revealed to me.

The telephone call was perplexing. I decided to get in my

car and take a drive. I was obviously creating some unintended anxiety in his church. I began praying and asking God to show me the answer. Within minutes, these words suddenly came to mind; *A great sign appeared in the sky, a woman clothed with the sun, with the moon under her feet and on her head a crown of twelve stars.* I knew this was from the book of Revelation. Another passage suddenly went through my mind: *Then afterward I will pour out my spirit upon all mankind. Your sons and daughters shall prophesy, your old men shall dream dreams, your young men shall see visions; even upon the servants and handmaids in those days, I will pour out my spirit.*

I sped back home, picked up my Bible and turned to the Book of Revelation and found the passage in Chapter 12. It took a little longer but the other passage was finally identified as Joel, Chapter 3. With Bible in hand I quickly dialed the pastor's number. "I asked God to give me an answer to your request and I believe He has." He thanked me after I read the passages to him over the phone.

Later that week, I received another call from him asking if I would meet with his church board and explain my trip. I was to meet with them the following evening. I prayed and asked God to please allow me to say only what I needed to say, and to help me be open to them. At that instant I heard some of the words reiterated from my Easter, 1983, encounter. "I WILL DEFEND YOU AT ALL TIMES. I WILL COME TO YOU AS MY SON." I believed I knew what it meant. Would I need the strength of those words for this meeting?

The following evening is etched clearly in my mind. I drove to the church and the pastor greeted me warmly at the door. He thanked me for coming and escorted me to what appeared to be a large conference room.

I counted twelve people seated at the conference table. The pastor very politely introduced me and we greeted each other. The person seated closest to me asked if I would be willing to share my recent trip with these board members. I nodded and began speaking. "I have just experienced what I believe to be a tremendous outpouring of the Holy Spirit in a small village called Medjugorje, in Yugoslavia (now Bosnia). My mother and I visited where it is believed that Mary, the mother of Jesus, is appearing to six young children. I have experienced something so powerful, that it left me, a quiet observer, virtually no doubt about its truth. I believe that God has sent the Virgin Mary as a messenger to this world. Her message is one of love and peace. She says that all are her children. She is asking for simple conversion of heart."

One person asked, "Is this like the Transfiguration?" I said "John, in Revelation, Chapter 12 says; 'A great sign appeared in the sky, a woman clothed with the sun and the moon under her feet, and on her head a crown of twelve stars.' If you read further in this chapter, you will see this is undeniably Mary." I proceeded to describe how the young visionaries saw her every day with the twelve stars around her head. I then quoted the passage in Joel, Chapter 3, that referred to young men seeing visions. As I was speaking, it occurred to me they knew very little of Our Lady's visits throughout apparition history.

"So you do truly believe what is happening there?" someone asked. I replied, "From my own personal experiences I very much believe what is happening there, but the Catholic Church is very slow to judge these matters until usually long after they have ended."

Another person said, "Don't you know Satan can disguise himself as an angel of light?" I replied that I knew Satan could deceive even the strongest of believers. I suggested since Mary, herself, says her enemy is Satan, perhaps they should reassess who she is within the Christian faith. "Does not Scripture say Mary was overshadowed by the Holy Spirit to bring Jesus into this world?"

When there was no reply I continued, "I believe we all realize God could have brought His Son here as a great king of royalty, as many believed He would come. God had a different Kingship planned for His Son and that plan involved a virgin birth from a young maiden. Gentlemen, Mary was literally fused with the Holy Spirit to bring Jesus into this world. She was never de-fused. When she is reportedly seen today, it is always in a great sphere of light. I believe this is the light of the Holy Spirit. One needs only to study all the Catholic Church-approved places she has appeared and then follow the many reported appearances in the last couple of decades like the Ukraine; Rwanda, Africa; Medjugorje, Yugoslavia, and especially Zeitoun, Egypt. There, a hundred thousand people or more watched her for hours at a time. In every appearance Mary is reported to be surrounded by great light. Her message is generally the same. She is always pointing us to her Son, Jesus. Why would Satan want to disguise himself as Mary when all she appears to want to do is bring us closer to Jesus, the Father, and the Holy Spirit? No, this surely is the Mother of God, the Virgin Mary, and she is functioning as God's messenger through the power of the Holy Spirit to remind us, once again, of the importance of God. Even Jesus Himself said to His apostles before His ascension into heaven, '*I have told you this while I am with you. The Advocate, the Holy Spirit that the Father will send in my name - He will teach you everything and remind you of all that I told you.*' The Spirit of Truth comes amongst us today through Mary and her spouse, the Holy Spirit. I pray that God will help you comprehend this. Yes, I believe in this event, for experiencing it has brought me closer to God than I have ever been in my life."

Then someone asked, "Do you believe in the beads?" "You mean the rosary?" I asked, as I pulled one out of my pocket. I held the rosary up in my hands for everyone to see. "I believe you are all grounded in Scripture here, and I respect you deeply for that. This is a Scriptural prayer. If you analyze these prayers, you will find they originate in Scripture. *The Lord's Prayer* was taught by Jesus, Himself. *The Hail Mary* was fashioned from the words of the Archangel Gabriel in Luke's Gospel. Yes, I do believe in these scriptural prayers. The beads are simply markers for the specific prayers."

After this, one man at the end of the table said, "I'm not sure it's healthy for you to continue singing here any longer." A second person said, "We've heard enough. Thank you for coming." I replied, "Thank you and God bless you all," before quietly leaving the room. As I walked away, I told God I would accept the fate of not singing with the choir again if that be the case. I was a servant of Jesus and Mary and there would be no more compromise with my faith. Yes, I was different. I came away sensing that I had probably stirred up a little problem for the pastor who had befriended me, but it was time to defend my faith and I would strive to do so from that moment until eternity. Another of the passages of the 1983 experience echoed in my mind: "I WILL PREPARE YOU WITH WORDS OF POWER...I WILL LEAD YOU IN ALL THINGS. WHEN YOU DO NOT KNOW WHAT TO SAY, I WILL COME TO YOU."

I walked away thanking the Holy Spirit for empowering me with the words that had come so easily to me. I was sad that one door was possibly closing, but I reminded myself that an entirely new chapter in my life was about to unfold. It was also sad for me in trying to comprehend that any Christian faith would not want to accept Mary as an intercessor to Jesus. What family is complete without its mother? Determination and courage were building. I knew I could no longer be hiding my light under a bushel basket, but the time had come for it to shine brightly to the entire world. With that, Respond Ministry was formed in my mind. Now I just had to bring the conceptualized non-profit apostolate into reality.

CHAPTER 8

We should submit our reason to the truths of faith with the humility and simplicity of a child.

St. Alphonsus Liguori

CONFIRMATION

With a fervor I completed a rough demo of the song I had been given that special morning in Yugoslavia, "The Lady of Medjugorje." Since I knew nothing about recording studios in Des Moines, I looked in the yellow pages and called the first one listed. Rick Condon, the studio engineer took my call. I explained to him that I would like to record a song and possibly a collection of songs. It had been approximately fifteen years since I had any serious involvement with music. I told him the song was the result of an inspiration and spiritual experience. Rather than dismissing me as too "off the wall" as I half-expected, he wanted to know more and expressed an interest in hearing the song. I told him I would drop off the demo at his studio later in the day. For the next couple of nights I wondered if I had done the right thing. This was all so implausible. I decided to go to Kansas City, Missouri, to ice skate and just get away for awhile. Having grown up in the Northeast, I loved to ice skate. Besides, I thought the three-hour drive from Des Moines to Kansas City would allow time to pray, think, and reflect on everything. I had been praying consistently that somehow God would confirm to me that I should continue with this idea of recording the music.

Immediately after the 4:30 p.m. Mass I left for Kansas City. It was a beautiful Saturday night in mid December. Once I arrived at the ice arena, all I could think about was the song and the words spoken to me in Medjugorje. It was a crisp, clear night and this outdoor skating arena was a wonderful place to relax. It was a pleasant surprise to see two Catholic sisters on the ice with a group of young children. I was prompted to skate up to them. I introduced myself as being from Des Moines and asked the sisters if they had heard of Medjugorje. Surprisingly, they had. Immediately I was enthused. I mentioned I had just returned from a pilgrimage there and found myself relaying the story about receiving music. The sisters seemed excited about my journey. I asked them if they wanted to hear the song I had received. They both enthusiastically nodded their heads. I had brought my micro-cassette player so I could listen to "The Lady of Medjugorje" as I skated. I pulled the recorder out of my pocket and played the song. When the song ended, the two sisters were looking at me with tears streaming down their cheeks. They both remarked that it sounded heaven-sent and encouraged me to follow God's leading. Their reaction provided another humbling glimpse of the power of the song. Had God arranged this unlikely meeting to provide confirmation to record "The Lady of Medjugorje"?

It was getting late and I thanked the sisters for listening and for their kind comments. I was faced with a three hour drive back to Des Moines and it was already around 9:30 p.m.

I was on the interstate approximately an hour from Des Moines when I finished praying the joyful, sorrowful and glorious mysteries of the Rosary and asking for the Blessed Mother's intercession to know what to do. Suddenly, I found myself saying out loud words that were running through my mind. The first sentence immediately caught my attention because I didn't understand its meaning. A tremendous sense of peace blanketed me as the words continued. I quickly pulled over to the side of the Interstate highway and turned on my inside dome light so truckers and passing cars could see me. Frantically I searched for paper and a pencil. In my excitement I totally forgot I had my micro recorder. I found a pencil in the glove compartment, but I couldn't find paper. I quickly tore two bank deposit slips out of my checkbook. I wrote the first two sentences down and paused to hear the rest. The words continued with each line coming like a ticker tape. I wrote down every word line by line. For about ten minutes I remained on the shoulder of the highway where tractor-trailers would pass every few seconds and shake the car. It was dangerous, but I couldn't stop writing. Finally the words came to an end. I hurriedly placed the deposit slips in my pocket and resumed my trip.

It was 1:00 a.m. when I arrived home. On preparing for bed I was reminded of the writing. I sat at my dining room table and began transcribing the deposit slips onto notepaper. In my concern over the situation on the highway, I had not paid full attention to the meaning of the words. It occurred to me it was a song and, as I began to rewrite the lyrics sentence-by-sentence, tears fell to the paper. The words confirmed to me that I was being called to be a servant. With courage and love I was to convey the words THEY were placing in my hands. This was one of the most overwhelming and unforgettable experiences thus far in my spiritual walk. Up to this point everything seemed to be very private. Now, however, God seemed to be asking me to be a servant and to pass on to others what I was being given. At this moment all doubts left me as to what I should do. With "The Servant" God was showing me the significance of these times. He was now directing me to help prepare other hearts and minds to trust in Him. I was being prepared for the mission ahead- to help lead others into His merciful arms.

The Servant
(To The World I)

Here's where I have you, where the sea meets the sand
To give my words to them I place in your hands
Be not troubled; be not afraid
For this I have called you, for this you've been made

I'm calling to all as time closes in.
It's time to prepare, My heart calls you in
Like sheep I have known each one by name
Do not waste time; come now in My name

Chorus:
Carry these words with courage, with courage and love
Tell them all they come; they come from above
This world I do see; this world I have known
It's for you that I come with great glory as told

It is your heart that needs purified
This world I have known, for this I have died
To be truly free you must do the same
It's time that you trust now in My name

It's to the cross that all now must come
Come while you can to Jesus my Son
Do not waste time; come be purified
Life will be restored, for you He has died

Repeat chorus.
Carry these words with courage...

Do not question why this time is at hand
For it is not now, that you'll understand
This is the time, as time presses on
This time was foretold by My servant John

Carry these words with courage...

This song reinforced the possibility that we could, indeed, be in the days mentioned in Chapter 3 of the prophet
Joel and again in Chapter 2 of Acts. If we are in those proph-
esied days, there would be an outpouring of Holy Spirit
upon many servants and handmaidens. The awareness of
being called to be a servant was imminent and the responsibility to "tell them all" became a sobering and serious responsibility.

*You whom I have called my servant, whom I have cho-
sen and will not cast off - Fear not, I am with you; be not
dismayed; I am your God. I will strengthen you, and help
you, and uphold you with my right hand of justice.* (Isaiah.
41: 9-10)

1

2

3

4

5

6

7

8

9

10   11   12

13   14   15

1. Jerry at the foot of the cross on Mt. Krizevac (Cross Mountain)
2. Pilgrims climbing Mt. Kricivac
3. Fr. Jozo laying on of hands
4. Jerry with Vicka Iivankovic
5. Recording *To The World* - Jerry, Regina, Jim and Kyle Clark
6. Recording "The Lady of Medjugorje" (trumpet)
7. Mother Angelica interview
8. Jerry singing "Say Yes"
9. The Heartland of America Marian conference
10. *To The World* placed at Mary's feet in St. James choir loft
11. Singing "The Lady of Medjugorje" in St. James Church
12. Jerry and Fr. Philip Pavich
13. Jerry, Andrea (Jerry's mother) and Claudette
14. Fr. Svetozar in war-torn Bosnia
15. Our Lady of Medjugorje statue in Medjugorje

Grace

Grace is first and foremost the gift of the Spirit who justifies and sanctifies us. But grace also includes the gifts that the Spirit grants us to associate us with his works, to enable us to collaborate in the salvation of others and in the growth of the Body of Christ, the Church. There are *sacramental graces,* gifts proper to the different sacraments. There are furthermore *special graces,* also called *charisms* after the Greek term used by St. Paul and meaning "favor", "gratuitous gift", "benefit". Whatever their character - sometimes it is extraordinary, such as the gift of miracles or of tongues - charisms are oriented toward sanctifying grace and are intended for the common good of the Church. They are at the service of charity which builds up the Church.

CHAPTER 9

Those who are led by the Holy Spirit have true ideas;
that is why so many ignorant people are wiser than the
learned. The Holy Spirit is light and strength.

St. John Vianney

HELPERS COME FROM
EVERYWHERE

E arly the next afternoon I was driving by my parish
church, St. Theresa's, which was only a few blocks
from my home. I felt prompted to stop and share my
pilgrimage experience with the priest before he went home
from celebrating the 11:30 Mass. I went into the church
and glanced around the sacristy where I thought I might
find him, but he had already left. On my way out I noticed
two young women praying. It was thirty minutes after Mass
had ended and they were the only other people in church.
The thought occurred to me they might have been to
Medjugorje. Why else would someone stay after Mass and
pray this long? Most people usually exit as soon as Mass is
over. I stopped at their pew, excused myself, and asked if
they had been to Medjugorje. They looked puzzled so I
quickly apologized and walked on down the aisle. Immedi-

ately one of the two women got up and followed me. She asked if I worked with the RCIA program (Right of Christian Initiation for Adults - the process whereby adults enter the Catholic Church.) When I had asked about Medjugorje earlier she thought perhaps I meant "Mystagogy," which is the last stage of the RCIA process. Her friend was thinking of becoming a Catholic and she thought I might be able to provide some information. I must have looked puzzled because she said, "What did you ask us?" I turned and responded, "I asked if you had been to Medjugorje. It's a small village in Yugoslavia where Mary, the mother of Jesus is appearing to six children." I could see the immediate interest in this woman's eyes. I told her my name and she introduced herself as Regina Myers from Kirksville, Missouri. She was visiting her friend, Susan, who had moved to Des Moines a few months before. Being non-Catholic and unfamiliar with Des Moines, Susan had unknowingly taken them to St. Theresa's Church rather than the church they had set out to find for the noon Mass. When they entered St. Theresa's by mistake, the 11:30 Mass was more than half over, so they decided to stay afterward and spend some time praying and reading the day's Scripture passages.

Susan joined us and we all walked to the back of the church. They wanted to know more about the small village. I proceeded to describe some of the experiences on my pilgrimage there. I mentioned the music I had received. They seemed very interested in the song "The Lady of Medjugorje." Since I lived just a few blocks from the church, I invited them to follow me to my home. I wanted to give them some literature about Medjugorje and play the song for them. They probably wondered what kind of guy would ask two strange women to his home. However, they must have sensed I was genuine and agreed to follow me down the street.

Minutes later we were in my living room. Regina noticed on the wall a large picture I had photographed in Medjugorje and exclaimed, "I've been there!" "How could you?" I said, "This was taken in Medjugorje." It was a picture of the Blue Cross taken in the early morning sun on Apparition Hill. (It's the striking photo I ended up using for the cover of the first *To The World* collection of music.) The young woman was somewhat shaken as she briefly described a personal experience a few years earlier at a shrine of Our Lady in Missouri. The picture, with the shaft of light streaming down on the cross had reminded her of this experience.

Not wanting to waste their time, I played the demo tape of "The Lady of Medjugorje". Before the song was over they were both in tears. I explained how I had received it and the instructions to prepare the song. Regina was visibly moved and abruptly said, "I'm supposed to sing with you." I was taken by surprise. She continued on to say she just felt she was somehow supposed to be involved in the project. Susan then explained that Regina had a wonderful voice and that I should hear her sing. Regina said she would be singing the next week at Midnight Mass in Edina, Missouri, if I had any interest in hearing her voice. I sensed something special with this woman. In fact, before they left the house, I told her I believed she had the heart of Our Lady. She said that was the most wonderful compliment she had ever been given and that her name, Regina Marie meant "Queen Mary." Her family had prayed the Rosary every night during her childhood and her father had a great devotion to Our Lady. I told her we would have to see what God had in store.

The next day Rick, the studio engineer, called me to say he liked the rough demo of "The Lady of Medjugorje" and felt he could put me in touch with a very talented and gifted arranger who was very spiritually-minded. He said he had been listening quietly over and over to the demo of the song. He was intent on analyzing it from a production point of view to determine how it could be made to "hook" the listener. In attempting to compare the song to other dramatic sound tracks, such as "Ben Hur" or "The Ten Commandments", he explained he wasn't finding any particular formula. Then, suddenly, as if out of nowhere, the thought entered his mind that the voice of Mary should be heard somewhere in the song, possibly toward the end. He said he was completely covered with chills when the thought entered his mind. I certainly knew what that meant, as chills seemed to be the litmus test for something heaven-sent. I told Rick "peace, peace, peace" was one of Our Lady's early messages to the visionaries. "Rick, I'm not sure, but I might have just met the woman who is supposed to do this." I told him I would let him know later.

My conversation with Rick prompted the decision to go to Missouri to listen to Regina sing. I called her to make arrangements to attend midnight Mass. She was very gracious and invited me to spend Christmas at her family farm where her parents still lived. She thought I would love her family and the simplicity of the farm. I conveyed to her that I would listen to her sing and I would then pray to determine whether we would try recording something in the studio. She expressed a willingness to be open and to help in any way she could.

It was cold and crisp on Christmas Eve when I arrived in the small town of Edina, Missouri, in time for the Midnight Mass. The historic St. Joseph's Church was unbelievably beautiful. Although a large church for such a small town, it was packed. I immediately noticed a beautiful full-sized statue of Our Lady to the left of the altar. Regina's beautiful solo during the Mass stirred my senses. I kept looking at the statue of Our Lady and listening to this woman singing, as if I were waiting for some kind of message. Suddenly, I knew in my heart Regina would be involved in this recording project. Like so many other coincidences, I was amazed I had met this woman in Des Moines, accidentally, in St Theresa's Church. Now, a short week later I was in a small Missouri town for who knows what? Once again I was humbled and in awe of how God seemed to be working.

Regina had told me Christmas Eve was her birthday, so I gave her a blue rosary which I had purchased in Medjugorje. I will never forget the time with her family at the farm in Edina. It was like Christmas at *The Waltons*; one of the simplest and holiest Christmases I could remember. The rural setting reminded me of Medjugorje. While I was there, I explained to Regina what the studio engineer had heard while studying the song. We needed someone to represent the voice of Mary at the end of the song and we would like to try her voice in the studio. I told her I also felt she was supposed to try the song "I'm in Love." This was the song I had written that related to the Matthew Chapter 6:24 verse. I felt this song would be better sung as a duet. She agreed to come to Des Moines and help me with the project. Her brother, Jim Clark, and his wife Kyle, led the beautiful midnight Mass choir and were also very talented. I invited them to be involved as well and to assist in background vocals.

In the next couple of weeks Rick introduced me to the musical arranger. I felt a real connection with this Christian man. Without reservation, I was able to communicate the story of Medjugorje and my own personal experiences leading up to this title song. He was one of the most talented pianists and arrangers I would ever meet. Although not Catholic, he immediately tuned into the essence and meaning of the music and, moreover, was very sensitive to my story. The tremendously creative rapport between Rick and this arranger was the final piece needed to begin the project.

The decision to record an entire collection of songs came as a result of quietly praying and reflecting on the beginning words of the message heard in St. James Church in Medjugorje; "COME SING MY SONGS TO ME. COME SING MY SONGS FOR ME." I believe the Holy Spirit helped me understand that these first few words of the message referred to many of the songs I had previously written. For these were the songs I received over time which I had so privately coveted. It was also then that I arrived at the title of the collection. I had examined again the words "WHEN COMPLETED, RETURN AND PLACE IT BEFORE MY FEET TO BE ANOINTED AND BLESSED BEFORE IT GOES OUT **TO THE WORLD!**" The title would be *To The World.* But would the world ever hear this music? I could only trust these words meant what they said.

Many of the arrangements would call for members of the Des Moines Symphony Orchestra to participate. The cost of the project would be a considerable risk, but I quickly realized there was no more important risk than to risk for God. If I believed what I had heard, then I had to carry this out with faith. The cost of the project scared me a little. I had my father's inheritance money set aside in a safe place. I had always promised myself it would only be used for a purpose that would have pleased him. I knew now I would be using that money to complete this project. I had a real sense of peace with this decision. I knew in my heart and mind that even if this music went no further than the confines of my home, I had to follow the instructions heard in Medjugorje.

We began the recording sessions with a strong team that had been assembled with almost no effort on my part: an extremely talented studio engineer, a wonderful Christian arranger, great studio musicians and talented, spiritual vocalists. Even my nephew, Todd, flew in from Fitchburg to play the piano on several songs. I asked a local religious community of sisters to pray for this project and felt covered in prayer. I also invited a good friend of mine, Jennifer, to come to the recording sessions to lend prayer support. She was a source of encouragement and believed in what I was doing.

This was my first attempt at anything of this magnitude. Many times I felt like Peter in Holy Scripture. I felt like I was trying to walk on the water toward Jesus in the middle of a storm, and I knew I couldn't look anywhere but straight ahead. I had to be faithful and keep my focus.

Trust in the Lord with all your heart, on your own intelligence rely not; In all your ways be mindful of Him and He will make straight your path. (Proverbs. 3: 5-6)

CHAPTER 10

Humility, humility and always humility. Satan fears and trembles before humble souls. The Lord is willing to do great things, but on condition that we are truly humble.

Servant of God, Padre Pio

WONDERS OF GRACE

W e kept up a hectic pace with recording and by mid-February, 1989, the recording project was nearly complete. Several events I will never forget took place during the production of the *To The World I* collection.

Every time I sing "Lovely, Lovely Lady" I can still visualize what I saw in my home on that particular morning in early February. After each recording session I would ask for a demo tape of the latest song so I could go home and quietly study it for any flaws. One morning, as usual, I was preparing to go to work. I placed the tape recorder in the bathroom so I could listen to the demo of "Lovely, Lovely Lady" we had recorded the night before. My face was fully lathered with shaving cream and I had just begun to shave. I was wondering if Our Lady was happy with this song. The words and music surrounded me but, suddenly, I was no longer looking into the mirror. I was peering through a window into a very plain room with white walls. In this room was a young girl, about thirteen or fourteen years old. She wore a full-sleeved, white smock that reached down to her feet and tied around her waist. Her feet were in sandals. I could see the straps and other distinct features. Because of the stark, white surroundings, her facial features were very noticeable. Her hair was dark and her complexion was very pale except for the rosy patches on her cheeks. From my perspective, I could not tell her eye color, but with the eyebrows and lashes, they appeared dark. Amazingly, the young girl was looking in my direction, smiling the entire time and dancing to the rhythm of "Lovely, Lovely Lady." I remember the distinctive dance clearly. It was like a sixties flashback to a dance called the "Freddie." She would lift up her arm and leg together on one side, then the other. This continued in rhythm with the song. She just kept smiling. Her smock would lift up when she lifted her leg. She moved only a little bit from the center of the room. I don't know how long this lasted, but when the music ended I came back to reality with a humbling realization. This unusual encounter was surely another grace of God. In my heart I knew He was telling me Mary was pleased with the song.

(Recently, I was provided one of many confirmations to write this book when I came across an old book <u>St. Therese of the Child Jesus</u>. The book described a strange malady that befell Therese as a young girl in 1883.

"And how great was the grief of M. Martin at the thought of losing his "little queen". He arranged to have a Novena of Masses for her in the sanctuary of Our Lady of Victories, in Paris.

At the invalid's bedside stood a statue of Our Lady, which had always been venerated by the family. During the novena at an unusually violent crisis, Marie, Leonie and Celine, in tears, beside their little sister's bed, addressed their supplications to it.

Near to dying grief, Therese was to relate, "I also had turned towards my heavenly Mother, beseeching her with all my heart to have pity on me. Suddenly, the statue came to life! Our Lady became beautiful, so beautiful that I shall never be able to find words to describe the divine beauty. Her countenance shone with ineffable sweetness, goodness, tenderness, but what stirred me to the very depths of my soul was her dazzling smile!" Little Therese was well again. This miracle happened on the 13th of May, 1883."

This excerpt from the book, published in 1955, brought me to my knees when I saw the accompanying picture of St. Therese's statue of Our Lady. Eight years had passed since the experience with "Lovely, Lovely Lady" in my bathroom. The picture of Our Lady's statue in the old book was similar to the girl who was smiling and dancing to that song. The distinctive details of her smock and sandals were identical. St. Therese has surfaced many times in my journey of grace.)

Another unforgettable event happened in that same month. This incident, however, was dark and insidious. Rick, the studio engineer, was excellent at mixing all the sound tracks and directing the recording project. One night I asked him where he kept the master tapes. I wondered if the tapes were insured in the event of a fire. He said he couldn't answer that question but assured me nothing had ever happened in all the years he had worked at the studio. I cautioned that everywhere Our Lady's work was being done the enemy was also there attempting to ruin it. He was amazed when I said this, but did not seem overly concerned. Shortly after that, we recorded "The Servant," the special song I had received before Christmas on my way back from skating in Kansas City.

Many hours of preparation had gone into this song and the final result was glorious beyond my expectations. The essence of the song and message had been captured superbly. I had just conveyed to Rick that I didn't think I could ever sing "The Servant" that well again. After laboring on the intricate final mix, we decided to take a half-hour break and get a bite to eat. On returning to the studio I told Rick I would meet him inside in a couple of minutes as I had to get something out of my car. When I walked into the studio, I found Rick sitting dejectedly with his head in his hands. Visibly distraught, he told me to look in the corner of the studio behind me. I turned and could hardly believe my eyes. All over the floor were strewn thousands of minute strands of tape. In our absence the master tape of the collection had been spinning furiously and knocking off bits of tape every time it turned around. It was a strange and eerie sight. I immediately felt the work of an enemy. I sensed this must be an important project for the enemy to want to destroy it. I could tell from Rick's reaction, the situation was serious. "What does this mean, Rick?" He said he wasn't sure yet, but that several songs could be gone.

Surely all the hours, all the preparation, all the money invested could not be destroyed in a mere thirty minutes. I told Rick I had to go for a walk. My worst fears had come true. I was too disturbed to stand there looking at the remnants of this special project scattered all over the studio floor. I remember asking God as I walked outside how this could happen. About ten minutes later I returned to the studio. Rick had called the owners to come and see what had happened. When they arrived, they were astonished by what they saw. The owners of the studio said there was no physical explanation for what had happened. They had never seen anything like this before.

Rick had assessed the damage to the master tape and was praying we might be lucky. It appeared that only the last half of "The Servant" was ruined. The owners offered to pay to re-record and re-engineer that song. Fortunately, all of the singers and musicians agreed to return over the next few nights. This was no small feat considering the hectic schedules of the musicians and the fact that the background vocalists lived three and a half hours away in Missouri. Heaven must have been with us though because the second version of "The Servant" ended up even better than the one destroyed.

During the early weeks of the recording sessions Jennifer suggested I meet with a friend of hers, Father Frank Bognanno, who served as Chancellor for the Diocese of Des Moines. She was convinced he would like my story and music and arranged an appointment for us to meet. We arrived at the Chancery a few evenings later. I brought a portable tape recorder and the demo version of "The Lady of Medjugorje." After Jennifer introduced me to Father Bognanno, I relayed my story and then played the tape. He commented that he loved it and went on to say, "Mother Angelica would probably like to hear this." I said "**Who**?" he repeated, "Mother Angelica." "How do you know her?" I asked. Turning to Jennifer he said, "Didn't you tell Jerry about my television work?" Jennifer apologized and said she had totally forgotten. I told Father that on my return flight from Medjugorje I sang this song on the plane without accompaniment and someone yelled out, 'I'll see you on <u>Mother Angelica</u>." "Would you like to be on her show?" he asked. I couldn't believe what I was hearing as he explained he hosted a series called <u>The Vineyard</u> on her Eternal Word Television Network. "I'll see if I can arrange with

Mother for you to be on her show." I was stunned as I heard him continue. "I'll call you tomorrow. If Mother consents, I will let you know what the producer needs." As we walked out of the office I was in awe. Jennifer knew, but had forgotten about Father Bognanno's professional relationship with Mother Angelica.

The next day Father Bognanno called to confirm that I would appear on <u>Mother Angelica's show</u>. On February 14th, 1989, Valentines Day, a day I will always remember, I sang "The Lady of Medjugorje" and was interviewed by Mother Angelica on EWTN. I gave a brief overview of how I had received the song. It wasn't until later I learned that her show reached over fifteen million viewers. After this appearance on Mother's show my phone in Des Moines started ringing. People began ordering the music and I was invited to present my witness and songs in numerous churches throughout the country.

After hearing me sing the "Lady of Medjugorje" on EWTN, a representative from Queen of Peace Ministries in South Bend, Indiana, called the network inquiring how to reach me. I returned the call and was invited to sing at the first National Medjugorje Conference to be held in May, 1989, at Notre Dame University. I sang only "The Lady of Medjugorje." Singing this one four-minute song at that national conference resulted in numerous invitations to subsequent Catholic conferences throughout the country to sing and also to give witness. Respond Ministry was now a reality.

(One of those conferences was the Wichita Marian Conference in 1990. I was struck by the holiness of that event. After my presentation, one of the young visionaries from Medjugorje walked up to me, handed me his rosary and said, "Jerry, my brother!" My heart was so moved. This same rosary turned gold before the week's end. Another heartfelt experience happened at that conference. Father Svetozar Kraljevic, the Franciscan priest from Medjugorje, whose book was instrumental in guiding me to make the pilgrimage with my mother, was one of the speakers. After my presentation he approached me with a hug, looked into my eyes and with his broken English said, "Keep singing, just keep singing. You are a prophet in our times." God's mercy was great to allow me to meet these two special individuals whom I admired and respected so much. Our paths would cross in love many times thereafter.)

Regina lived three hours away in Missouri and made several trips to Des Moines to work on the project. The morning after recording "I'm In Love" she was once again on the road returning to Kirksville, Missouri to get to work. She reached in her purse for the blue and silver rosary I had given her as a birthday present on Christmas Eve. She glanced down as she began to pray and nearly drove off the highway when she saw gleaming gold on that rosary which had been silver the evening before in the studio. It was her sign that Our Lady was pleased.

We were on the final few songs of the *To the World* collection when Rick informed me that we had enough time on the master for one more song. I prayed and asked God's help in deciding what should be recorded.

Someone commented to me that I should consider recording "The Lady of Medjugorje" as a simple instrumental to close the collection. As a tribute to my father, I decided to record a trumpet solo over the haunting instrumentals of the song.

For many years after college, I made my living as a performer - singing and playing the trumpet in a show band. During the big band era of the 1940's my father had also been a professional trumpet player. When he passed away, it was a devastating personal loss. It was odd that I was being prompted to play the instrumental on the trumpet. I hadn't played professionally for fifteen years. Even more interesting, I believed I was being prompted to play it with my father's trumpet.

It made no sense to want to play my father's trumpet. I was concerned after so many years whether I could play at all and whether I should be using my own horn. However, I called my mother and told her what I wanted to do. I hadn't been able to even look at my dad's trumpet since he died, so she was surprised but promised to send it immediately.

The morning I received his trumpet is clear in my mind. I slowly and reverently unwrapped the package and opened the case, handling the instrument like a piece of fine china. Here it was! Oh, the emotions that ran through me as I slowly picked it up. I gently carried it to the kitchen to polish it. My mother had told me many stories about my father and how much he loved his music. I knew he would have been so proud to hear this collection, especially this song for Our Lady.

I brought the trumpet into the living room and attempted to play it. I sounded terrible. Meanwhile Rick had called me that day to inform me we would record the final version of "The Lady of Medjugorje" the next night. I had less than twenty-four hours to become a trumpet player again. It was nearly impossible. Each hour that went by I would try to play for about ten minutes until my lip gave out. I went to bed that night thinking it was a noble idea but that it was just not realistic to think I could play the trumpet again after fifteen years.

The following day was Ash Wcdncsday. That evening we were scheduled to complete the *To The World I* recording. I arrived at the studio with ashes still on my forehead. Regina drove from Missouri and met us at the studio. She was scheduled to record the three words, "Peace, peace, peace", we had decided would be heard at the end of the song. I entered the studio and Rick began "The Lady of Medjugorje" for the final time. Regina was coached to say the words at the end of the song. It went perfectly and the song was completed and ready for the world.

I had taken my father's trumpet into the studio just to see if, by chance, I could play it. I tried warming up in the corner by playing musical scales. It sounded pretty rough. I approached the microphone in the studio and asked Rick if he would run the background track to the song one more time. I wanted to play along for a test. The music started. I closed my eyes and began to play. A few seconds into the song I opened my eyes and realized I was playing the trumpet effortlessly; the notes were flowing from my lips and my heart. I was dumbfounded but kept the presence of mind to continue playing. I felt as though my father was right there in the room with me. The tears started streaming down my face as I was playing; I thought, "Just a little more and I'm done." The song finished and I was driven to my knees. I knew I was experiencing another healing; I knew my dad was with me in this calling. Regina hurried into the sound room. She said that what had just happened was the most incredible thing she had seen yet. Unbelievably, she said,

"Your father must have been there beside you."

I walked into the mixing room and told Rick I didn't think I would be able to play that again. He said it wouldn't be necessary. He felt it was performed flawlessly. He had pushed the record button and, with that one take, the instrumental had been completed and the last song on the collection was in place.

The mysticism continued that night when I went home. I was praying at the small altar in my bedroom and listening to the finished trumpet version. As I sat quietly on my bed I again heard the soft voice. "THIS SONG, WITH THE TRUMPET, WILL ONE DAY BE HEARD THROUGHOUT RUSSIA AND WILL BE A SOURCE OF CONVERSION FOR MANY." I was completely awestruck. (If this is to happen it is yet to come!)

With the *To The World I* collection complete, the first person I sent it to was my mother. Soon after receiving it she called to ask who was playing the trumpet on the last song. When I told her it was me she couldn't believe it. "That wasn't you, I know your tone. That sounds exactly like your father." My brother also commented that it sounded exactly like my father playing. The entire family was in tears listening to the collection. Yes, perhaps my father *was* playing the trumpet. It certainly felt as though he was with me.

Also about this time I received a call from a friend in Kansas City. He heard there would be a Lutheran speaking about Medjugorje at a local Catholic church and thought I would want to come and listen. I asked Regina to go with me. The speaker's name was Wayne Weible. We were moved by the depth of love this messenger conveyed for Our Lady. I listened intently to his story and there were many similarities in how we had been called. I felt I needed to meet him and share my story. Perhaps he could help me know further what direction I needed to fulfill my mission. I made my way to the back of the church, introduced myself and explained in a nutshell what I had received in Medjugorje. His comment stayed with me. He said, "If you have received a mission from Our Lady, You don't need me. All you need to do is pray and fast and let her lead you. You will know what you have to do." I thanked him for, in my heart, I knew it was the right answer. (Little did I know in years to come that we would cross paths many times at numerous Marian Conferences throughout the country.)

Although I had sent the collection to my mother and numerous orders were coming in, I felt I had to fulfill the words heard in Medjugorje before any could be sent out. "WHEN COMPLETED RETURN AND PLACE IT BEFORE MY FEET TO BE ANOINTED AND BLESSED BEFORE IT GOES OUT TO THE WORLD." I knew I would have to return soon to that small village with the completed music in hand.

CHAPTER 11

Teaching unsupported by grace may enter our ears, but it never reaches the heart. When God's grace does touch our innermost minds to bring understanding, then His word, which is received by the ear, can sink deep into the heart.

St. Isadore of Seville

THE RETURN VISIT

Right away I made arrangements to return to Medjugorje in April. It seemed appropriate to find myself in that holy village on the feast of Divine Mercy. It was a magnificent trip.

Early in my visit, I sought out Father Philip Pavich, the English-speaking Franciscan priest who had inspired me so on my first visit. When we met, I had the *To The World I* music collection in my hands. I explained to him the words that I had heard on my initial trip and the reason for my return. It was the need to fulfill these words that had brought me back. He seemed interested and asked me to meet him in a few minutes.

Father Philip's office was a small makeshift trailer in the church courtyard. As I entered the sparsely furnished room, he invited me to be seated. He was curious about the picture on the front cover and the story of the music. He said he would play the songs later and let me know his reaction. He looked at me and began asking a series of personal questions. It took me by surprise when he asked me if he could hear my confession, but I quickly nodded my head.

A few minutes into my confession he asked if I had ever participated in any abortions. I told him yes, but that I felt forgiven from a previous confession. He looked at me with a deep seriousness and said, "I now want you to give these children names." In tears, I decided Mark and John would be their names. He said, "I want you to pray often to them by name and I want you to ask for their forgiveness." Thinking about these two little ones overwhelmed me with emotion. I had tried to bury this for so long and now they had names. The priest continued to probe my soul until virtually no stone was left unturned. Again the cleansing power of God was reaching into my being even more deeply than my first visit. The Holy Spirit, with the fire of His love, was burning like a furnace in my heart. God had worked very powerfully through Father Pavich. English-speaking pilgrims were always vying for this priest's attention. I felt tremendously blessed to have been given this much personal time with him.

The next day I saw Father Pavich in the courtyard. He approached me and asked if I could meet him at 5:30 p.m.. He pointed to a small door on the side of the church and told me to wait for him there. I wondered what he had in mind but I didn't hesitate to go back at the appointed time. At 5:30 Father arrived, quickly unlocked the door and instructed me to go up the winding stairs to wait for the visionaries. Before leaving he locked the door. I didn't question his directive. I followed the narrow staircase that led to the upper choir loft. As I reached the top of the stairs, I immediately noticed a large painting of the Blessed Virgin Mary on the far wall. I placed the *To The World I* album cover at the foot of this painting and then sat down and began quietly praying and thanking God for leading me and giving me this special grace.

Twenty minutes had passed when I heard the Rosary begin down in the main body of the church. After about twenty minutes more, I heard the click of the lock in the small door below. People were coming up the stairs. I recognized Marija Pavlovic and Ivan Dragicevic, two of the visionaries. They immediately went over and knelt before the large painting where the collection of music was placed. I watched intently and in awe as they experienced their visit with Mary. Part of the instructions heard on my first visit had now been fulfilled. The song had been placed before Our Lady's feet to be anointed and blessed. I felt the music could now go out to the world.

Two days later Father Pavich again recognized me in the crowd in the church courtyard. He approached me and asked if I would sing "The Lady of Medjugorje" as a communion meditation in St. James Church. His request came as a total surprise. I had not brought an accompaniment tape with me on the trip. It never occurred to me that I would need it. He said it didn't matter about the recorded instrumental. All he wanted was for me to sing the song from my heart like a prayer.

One of the pilgrims in our group overheard Father's request. He said he played the organ by ear and offered to accompany me. Trusting that somehow God would make this all work, I turned back to Father Pavich and conveyed I would be most honored to sing the "The Lady of Medjugorje" in the church.

The next morning we had only ten minutes in which to rehearse. I thought this would certainly be a minor miracle if this pilgrim truly could accompany me after having only ten minutes to listen and prepare. I was anxious and very nervous but trusted the Holy Spirit would help us.

Fr. Pavich finished Communion and nodded for me to sing. A hush came over the crowded church as the organist began playing a short introduction. As I looked down at the sea of faces one immediately stood out. Wayne Weible was sitting in the front pew! I closed my eyes and sang "The Lady of Medjugorje" from my heart. It was an overwhelming feeling. I had received my instructions in this very church and now I was singing the song live in front of God and this full church. When I finished, the church erupted in a thundering applause. I felt this as a time of incredible grace; a moment in time that I knew in my heart God and Our Lady certainly had ordained. I was filled with thanksgiving. Such love radiated in the church at that moment I felt that I had died and gone to heaven. After Mass, I quickly thanked the heroic organist and then a large crowd of people waited to greet me outside the church inquiring how they could get the music. I was amazed to find they were from all parts of the world. I was reminded of my original instructions, "BEFORE IT GOES OUT TO THE WORLD." It appeared this was also coming to pass. I was especially honored when Mr. Weible approached me to say he felt as though Our Lady was singing the song with me. Only a few months before in Kansas City, his words on the importance of prayer and fasting were imparted upon my heart and were vital for this mission.

I felt at the end of this trip that being in Medjugorje during the feast of Divine Mercy was no accident. I had once again received His loving mercy and another outpouring of grace. Again I marveled at the mysterious ways God works and wondered where the path would lead next.

CHAPTER 12

*No one is saved by his own strength, but he is saved
by the grace and mercy of God.*

St. Cyprian

AMAZING GRACE

On returning to the states, the graces continued. Invitations to give presentations at numerous Catholic churches and Marian conferences began to come in.

An extremely gifted videographer and friend, Bill Kuhn, who I later took to Medjugorje, helped me design a two hour multi-media concert presentation. His work was truly inspired. He had experienced something amazing in Medjugorje, although he was on the trip only to take photographs for the presentation. In Father Jozo's church he quietly positioned himself behind a pillar to be out of the way. While taking pictures he heard a voice say "DO YOU WANT TO OBSERVE OR DO YOU WANT TO PARTICIPATE?" He looked around the pillar to see who was talking to him, but no one was there. Father Jozo was laying hands on the hundreds present. Again, Bill heard the same words.

Almost involuntarily he left his camera position and proceeded in line for Father Jozo's blessing. The priest placed his hands on Bill's head and within seconds he was sprawled on the floor resting in the Spirit. This was a transforming moment for Bill. He explained that a bright light came into him at that moment Father Jozo began to pray. It literally knocked him out. He was shown later that the powerful light was Jesus.

After the first few presentations, especially when using Bill's visuals, I began to sense that my healing and conversion were being transmitted by the Holy Spirit from my heart into the hearts and minds of many listeners. The Holy Spirit seemed to be at work as the music would open them to listen and then Our Lady's message could be delivered. I could sense the shackles being removed from people right before my eyes. It appeared the message I had received in 1983 had come to life:

"YOU WILL DELIVER MANY.
YOU WILL SET FREE MANY CAPTIVES WHO ARE
   IMPRISONED AND IN CHAINS.
YOU ARE A STRONG ARM AND I WILL USE YOU.
AND YOU WILL CUT LIKE A TWO-EDGED SWORD.
WITHOUT EVEN KNOWING, YOU WILL SET THE
   ENEMY UNDER YOUR FEET."

It was a total surprise when a wonderful faith-filled couple, who believed in our mission, donated a fairly new van for our evangelization. With donated van and a multimedia concert presentation, I would find myself in the ensuing months travelling across the country to hundreds of churches and Catholic conferences and performing up to two-hour concert presentations. Everywhere we went we witnessed dramatic evidence of the Holy Spirit's transforming power.

*God added his testimony by signs, wonders, various
acts of power, and distribution of the gifts of the Holy Spirit,
according to His will.* (Acts. 2: 4)

The transforming effect was incredibly humbling. An inner sense that I was fulfilling my mission began to grow
within me. It was as if the power of God would come down
on an audience and literally take over the presentation. (It
is a tremendous grace to be invited to present my program
in Catholic churches, especially in the presence of the Blessed
Sacrament.) The Holy Spirit had impressed upon my heart
the importance of the presentations being held in the church
proper if possible. In this way, listeners whose faith had
weakened would be in a church if the Holy Spirit worked
life-changing power through the presentation and music.
They might then associate any personal conversion experience with being in the church and would possibly feel the
need to return.

We felt blessed when one of the Sisters of Mercy, who
we had asked to pray for our recording project, offered for
a short time to coordinate the hectic Respond Ministry
schedule and fill the many incoming orders. It was Sister
who later felt she discovered the meaning of the first two
lines of "The Servant." While praying and reading Holy
Scripture, she felt the Holy Spirit had directed her to the
last few lines of Chapter 12 in the Book of Revelation:

*Then the dragon became angry with the woman and
went off to wage war against the rest of her offspring, those
who keep the commandments and bear witness to Jesus. **It
took its position on the sand of the sea.***

Sister felt it meant that I was being placed in the front
lines to do battle. This passage of Scripture clearly described
Mary's offspring. those who keep the commandments and bear

witness to Jesus. I could not help ponder the wisdom of this passage. This one passage of scripture characterized all who were being called to bear witness to Jesus and the Kingdom with their lives. It was clear the battle could be expected. The messages the Blessed Virgin Mary was giving for the world were the keys to survival and protection. We would need all the spiritual armor possible. I could only trust in *Their* help and to live the messages of Medjugorje as faithfully as possible.

June 5, 1986: *Dear children, ...I am calling you to become active in living and carrying my messages to others. I desire that all of you become the living image of Jesus and bear witness to this unfaithful world...So be a light by the way you give witness with your lives. Thank you for having responded to my call.*

The Blessed Virgin Mary at Medjugorje

Being a part of the Marian conferences became especially fulfilling. An event that happened after a particular conference in Irvine, California, has never left my mind. When I returned home from that Spirit-filled conference, I received a call from a woman who had attended. She purchased a copy of the tape of my talk at the conference. She was prompted to call me to explain what had happened to her at her home. She explained that she was mowing the lawn while listening to my talk with headphones and a portable tape player. She said she listened to the entire tape and then felt compelled to listen to it a second time. She turned off the mower and went to sit quietly under a tree to listen again. She said the strangest thing happened to her when listening for the second time, and this was her reason for calling. I had talked about the purpose, healing and direction that took place on top of the mountain in Medjugorje. She went on to say she had a daughter with a learning disability and that the child learned best when she could associate meanings with acronyms or abbreviations. For example, her daughter was able to remember the archangels Michael, Gabriel, and Raphael by associating them with the abbreviation "Mgrs.," meaning God's managers. She said, "I heard the Holy Spirit tell me to tell you that God has given you your Ph.D. in spirituality." I wasn't sure how to respond. She said she hesitated to call me, but the prompting to do so was too overwhelming. I thanked her and said I would have to pray to assimilate the meaning of what she had heard.

In the days that followed, that conversation would not leave me. I found myself deeply pondering her words. I finally realized if God had given me a Ph.D. in spirituality, it wasn't due to anything I earned. This certainly was a different Ph.D. Perhaps I was to help others find their Ph.D. This simply meant helping others understand that surrender to God means allowing Him to lead one to his or her own personal purpose, healing and direction, hence, Ph.D.

During this time more songs were received, causing me to wonder if I was being prepared for a second collection. One was received while driving to Missouri to visit Regina. I had just prayed the Rosary and was thinking I would love to sing a song directed to Our Lady. I wanted it to be a song of gratitude to her for all the graces I was receiving. Within five minutes of my supplication, "You're My Lady" was received. What I was hearing was similar in style to "The Lady of Medjugorje" but was a more personal song from my heart. I was so graced to have received it.

114

You're My Lady
(To The World II)

You're my lady
In my heart I heard you call my name
O lady, because of you I'll never be the same
You took me by the hand
And showed me heaven's door
I've never known this kind of love before
O lady, I never thought that I could feel this way
O lady, now I know I want you here to stay
I followed what I heard
To half-way 'round the world
Now I know you mean the world to me

Instrumental...

O my lady, clothed with the sun
And crowned with stars so bright
O lady, with feet upon the moon that lights the night
You've helped me to see
What your Son means to me
Like you, I want to be within His light
You're my lady
This time on earth will one day pass away
O lady
My heart wants you to know and this I say
That while my time's at hand
With you I'll take this stand
And surrender all I am to Him today
And when my time is through
Then maybe I'll see too
This song for you was just the Father's plan.

Shortly after writing "You're My Lady", another song was received as a result of a supplication. I had asked for a song that would sum up the meaning of the events of Medjugorje. It was just as if The Blessed Virgin was speaking the words to me. It made me realize Regina would be singing this song with me also. I was so thankful for this blessing to write "Live The Message" as the very essence of Our Lady's visits in Medjugorje.

Live the Message
(To The World II)

If He's carried you this far, He'll carry you through
It's in His great power to do this for you
If you only will ask, just a question away

Be with me O Lord, be with me today
By the graces that flow, by the power above
Come to this mountain of love, and

Chorus:
Live the message
Live the message
Live the message that I send
Live the message
Live the message
Live it to the end

Your heart's like the soil for tilling anew
The message for hearing and planting it too
The winds come a blowin' to take it away

My love is a refuge, it's here you will stay
For He's giving the graces for me to say
This much I tell you to pray, and

Chorus:

Sometimes it's for planting, sometimes it's the rain
It can be sorrow and it can be pain
Decision's respected, it's all in your hands
Will you give to Jesus, surrender your plans?
It's for you that He died and wants to renew
Now it's all up to you

Chorus:

("Live The Message" would turn out to be my sister, Claudette's, favorite song.)

Our Lady and her spouse, the Holy Spirit, continued to reach into my soul. One of the most important promptings I received was to make closure on my first marriage, which had ended in divorce. This was a part of my life I didn't want to deal with again and an annulment had never seemed important. I had felt this prompting many times before, but somehow, someway, I would always convince myself it wasn't necessary. Now, however, the conviction to reconcile this aspect of my life was another fire burning in my heart. The difference this time was that I was fully desirous to carry out what I felt was being asked. I could see that this was my next step in the conversion process. I felt God would grant me the courage and grace necessary to be reconciled to Him and the Church.

With the guidance of my parish pastor, I followed through the long and tedious annulment process. When it was finally

117

granted, I felt another healing and a deeper liberation in my soul. Mysteriously on completion of the annulment, I received another song I would be most thankful for. Again in my mind I could hear Mary singing portions of the song. Her words of comfort were directed to me, to everyone.

I Will Never Let You Go
(To The World II)

You keep us in your mantle
You keep us safe and warm.
Your loving arms surround us
And you keep us free from harm
You will always keep us safely
Even when you find we stray
Your patience is amazing
You care for us this way

Chorus:

O you're a mother to us all
And our refuge is your love
You protect us when we're falling
And your love's sent from above
And you love us as your children
And because we trust you so
We will always hear you saying
I will never let you go

Now I say, dear children
That I want you all to see
I hold you oh so closely
Yes I hold you close to me

Live my message fully
Through each and every day
This will keep you safely
In my arms to stay

O I'm a mother to you all
And your refuge is my love
I'll protect you when you're falling
With my love sent from above
And I love you as my children
And because you trust me so
You will always hear me saying
I will never let you go

Oh you're a mother to us all
And our refuge is your love
You protect us when we're falling
And your love's sent from above
And I love you as my children
And because you trust me so
You will always hear me saying
I will never let you go

Interlude...

We can hear you softly saying
I will never let you go

Because of my deep sorrow for my earlier destructive decisions, the next song was a special gift. I had never received a song relative to the importance of life before, so "Say Yes" was particularly poignant for me. As a result of this song I was invited to sing at a national pro-life rally at the steps of the nation's Capital. Coincidentally, I had the wonderful privilege of being with Father Philip Pavich again, the priest from Medjugorje who asked me to name my two unborn sons. We were being called to give our talents as gifts for this important event. This was a cherished moment. I felt that when God granted this song to me, he was saying I was healed enough to now help others in their healing.

Say Yes
(To The World II)

Time can lead to a memory
A life brings a fullness to time
How can it be so many can't see
The gift that is yours and mine

Oh, what a lonely decision
Choosing the fate of a child
If that child were you, what would you say to do?
Here I am; can't you see I'm alive
Here I am; can't you see I'm alive!

Refrain:
Say yes, say yes to the great gift of life
It's the gift that we give to the world
Say yes, say yes to the great gift of life
Every child has a right to be heard
Say yes, say yes, leave it all in His hands
Life is all part of His master plan

A woman not so long ago
A mother, I'm happy to know
Faced with a choice, then she raised up her voice
She said yes and a child was born

And the child was Jesus, the Lord

Repeat Refrain
Say yes...

Being single and childless when this song was written, I often wondered if a child of mine would one day ever hear it. I knew when "Say Yes" was completed I would sing it wherever I would be sent. It has been humbling to witness so many tears and conversions while singing this song. We have received countless letters and have witnessed many conversions from people who have been touched deeply by its message.

(During concert presentations this is one of my favorite songs to sing because it provides an opportunity for women with newborn children or expectant mothers to give witness to their decision to say "Yes" to life.)

The songs just kept coming. "Living In The Light of Your Love" had as its Scriptural basis the verses of Matthew 6: 19-22 and John 8: 12.

Do not store up for yourselves treasures on earth, where moth and decay destroy, and thieves break in and steal. But store up treasures in heaven... The lamp of the body is the eye. If your eye is sound, your whole body will be filled with light. Matthew. 6: 19-22)

Jesus spoke to them again, saying, "I am the light of the world. Whoever follows me will not walk in darkness, but will have the light of life." (John 8. 12)

Living In The Light Of Your Love
(To The World II)

Chorus
I'm living in the light of Your love
Building up my treasures for Your Kingdom
Raptured by the sight of Your face
Now I'm all caught up in Your grace
And I'm living, Living in the light of Your love.

Yes I'm living in the light of Your love
Filling with Your light of love within me
Hearing all You send from above
And it's what I'm singing of
And I'm living, living in the light of Your love

I carry You close in my heart
Fears and worries no longer around
I'm trusting in You to see all this through
With a faith and new love that I've found

I don't need to understand the reasons
It really doesn't matter at all
Because Your love for me is all that I need
Now I'm giving back what You're sending down

Chorus

Now I'm standing here gazing at You
Hearing what You're saying to me
And what You're saying, I'm relaying
For the whole world to see

For it's time to understand the seasons,
Being watchful unto the night
It's time for praying, keep on praying
Coming closer into His light. Yes I'm...

Chorus

It seemed like a forgone conclusion to decide to compile a second collection of music, *To the World II*. We had begun recording when, on Holy Thursday, 1990, one of the most remarkable experiences took place. It was intense and unforgettable.

I was seated at my desk at work when a tremendous sense of peace blanketed me, which I can only liken again to a rapture. Suddenly, it was as though I was in a vision from an aerial perspective. The sensation was that of hovering over a desolate area of land. In the distance I could see what appeared to be three crucifixes. Quickly, the scenery changed and I found myself much closer to them. The scene changed again and I was looking up at a body on one of the crosses. The wind howled around me and I could feel the cold. The bloodied body on the cross was still alive. Every muscle was strained and every vein distended. The man was looking down at me. Struggling in the distress of gazing on this scene, my heart pained with indescribable anguish. I understood this must be Jesus in his death agony right before my eyes. Words began slowly running through my mind as I watched Him die. From whose perspective were these words? It seemed as if half of my brain was watching the vision and the other half was attempting to analyze the words and the why of it all. It was shocking to realize I was experiencing all of this horror through the eyes of Mary while standing before her dying Son. Then, strangely, I felt as if

I was inside of Mary while holding the dead corpse of her Son. I could hear her words and then I could hear the words spoken internally to her from Jesus. When the vision ended, my heart was on fire. I was shaken and wondering what had just happened. When I read the written words in totality, I had to leave my office. The experience was almost too much for me to handle. The sorrow that I felt for Mary was truly incredible. I realized I had been given a song and that the lyrics were remarkable. The experience was indescribable. I had felt I was not just there with Mary, but **inside Mary**.

It was impressed upon me that Regina should sing the voice of Our Lady in "At The Cross." She had been planning a trip to Medjugorje and felt that now her main reason for the trip had been revealed. She would go with an open heart to allow God and Our Lady to prepare her to sing this powerful song. In June, she was on her way with a group of pilgrims from Des Moines.

The week Regina returned from Medjugorje, I could tell that she had experienced a great deal of grace. She looked so peaceful and glowing. She said she had the privilege of having Father Pavich hear her confession. She commented that she had never felt such remorse for her sins and had experienced a powerful cleansing. The final recording sessions were scheduled for the following weekend. Regina felt she had done all she could to prepare to sing "At the Cross." It was obvious by her sense of peace that she had taken this preparation time very seriously.

I vividly recall watching her through the glass window in the studio as she held her Rosary tightly in her hands and then closed her eyes. Rick began to play the background accompaniment orchestration of "At The Cross." We watched in awe as we heard her voice soar to the heavens in song. Our hearts were deeply moved. I knew God had truly prepared her with the necessary graces to represent Our Lady's voice in this song.

Immediately after the session, Regina looked visibly shaken. She had just experienced a very unusual and mysterious sensation. As she began to sing she was praying and asking God to allow her voice to correctly represent Our Lady. A few moments into the song she had involuntarily imagined she was wearing a veil over her head and a long rough robe that fell to the floor. It was as though she was wearing Mary's clothes. The experience was unexpected and had totally unnerved her. It sounded similar to what I had experienced while receiving and writing the song. Rick commented that he felt that "At The Cross" was going to reach a lot of people in a very important way.

At The Cross
(To The World II)

At the cross the lonely sadness
Piercing to my very soul
Broken heart, despair and darkness
Oh the pain and now the cold
How could this all have happened
What had He ever done?
And now to see You dying
I'm dying too my Son

Where are all Your loved ones
Oh they've left us all alone
John and I stand side by side
And it seems so cold.
Soon it will be over

But the hardest part's to come
With one last breath
Give unto death
All, it seems is done

And they take Him off the cross
Oh and they bring Him here to me
As I hold Him in my arms
This voice is heard in me...

They'll be all called by you, mother
To a peace that lasts forever
If they all but join together
And unite with Me, your Son
It's the reason for My dying
Soon I'll take away your crying
And the fullness of My glory
They will all see soon again

We are all called by Our Mother,
To a peace that lasts forever
If we all but join together
And united with His Son
It's the reason for His dying
And salvation not denying
And the fullness of His glory
We will all see soon again...

We are all called by Our Mother
To a peace that lasts forever...
(fade)

The path of conversion was bringing me deeper. Once again
it had led me to the foot of the Cross. This mysterious song
nearly completed what was needed for the *To The World II*.

This song deeply affected Rick, the engineer. When we began the *To The World* project, he had been away from the Catholic Church for some years. The recording process spurred the beginning of a deep conversion which was fueled when his rosary turned gold during one of the recording sessions. (Rick and my friend Jennifer met during the *To The World I* project. They are now married and in the formation program for Rick to be ordained a deacon.)

Only one song was left to round out the collection. After the intensity of "At The Cross," the way the final song came about still makes me smile. We were performing a concert in a small Midwest town soon after we finished recording "At The Cross." I had conveyed to the audience part of the message heard in Medjugorje. "COME SING MY SONGS ...THE SONG WILL BE HEARD THROUGHOUT THE WORLD, EVEN IN DIFFERENT LANGUAGES..." After this particular concert a young Hispanic gentleman approached me and said, "I believe I'm supposed to translate 'The Lady of Medjugore' into Spanish." I immediately encouraged him to follow his prompting. Approximately two weeks later he presented me with the beautiful Spanish lyrics for Our Lady's song. With a great deal of coaching I was honored to sing the Spanish version of "The Lady of Medjugorje" as the last song on the *To The World II* collection.

A sense of God the Father's and Our Lady's love for all peoples intensified with the addition of the Spanish version. Where would the path lead now?

CHAPTER 13

Sometimes, when I read spiritual treatises...my poor little mind soon grows weary, I close the learned book which leaves my head splitting and my heart parched, and I take the Holy Scriptures. Then all seems luminous, a single word opens up infinite horizons to my soul.

St. Therese of Lisieux

THE BELLS AND ST. THERESE

By July, we were nearly finished recording *To The World II*. I had received an invitation in Des Moines to do a concert presentation in my own parish, St. Theresa of the Child Jesus. I was very tired from the recording sessions, working full time and doing concert presentations nearly every weekend. It was one of those times when doubt was creeping in as to how long I should, or could, keep doing these presentations. For as long as I live, I will never forget that night at St. Theresa's. Rick, the studio engineer was present. We had just finished recording "Living in the Light of Your Love" that afternoon so Regina, Jim and Kyle were there from Missouri too. I was looking forward to singing this new song for the first time that evening at St. Theresa's.

The main body of the church was full. The multimedia presentation was being performed as planned. I had just finished singing "Living in the Light of Your Love" and had reached the point where I quoted a message from Our Lady, *You are entering my times.* Suddenly, GONG! GONG! GONG! GONG! GONG! Bells began ringing everywhere. I made a comment to Rick that the bells sounded like the church bells of St. James Church in Medjugorje and that we should try to come here and record them. We had been trying to find the right ones for the song "I'll Never Let You Go".

We completed the first half of the presentation and had taken a short break. During this intermission, many of the parishioners came up to ask me if the bells were part of the presentation. When I shook my head many proceeded to tell me they had never heard those bells before and did not believe they were the bells of St. Theresa's. One lady said, "I live only three houses away. I have never, in my twenty years of being a member of this church, heard those bells before." A chill went up and down my spine. I knew what that chill meant!

We began the second half of the presentation and everything went as planned until we reached the song "The Servant". Half-way through the song, at the high point, the same bells began tolling again. When I looked out into the audience, many were in tears. Amazingly, the bells were in perfect tune with the music. What I noticed this time about the bells was that they sounded as though they were being heralded inside and outside of the church at the same time. Once the song was finished, I paused and asked how many people heard the bells during that song. Everyone raised their hand. Someone asked again if the bells were part of the recording. I shook my head and looked over to Rick, the studio engineer. He appeared shaken. He later told me he couldn't have planned for any bells to be so perfectly in tune with the music. Many listeners took their turn proclaiming that these were not the bells of St. Theresa's. I didn't want to spend time speculating so we continued on with the presentation.

When the concert was over, the associate pastor walked up to me from the back of the church as we were packing up our equipment. Shaking his head he said, "I don't know, I just don't know. I've never heard those bells before. I just don't know."

Afterwards, a group of people wanted to stay and pray. About twenty minutes later, while we were praying, the bells rang again. In the basement level, a reception was being held for anyone who had attended the concert. When we arrived at the reception many were talking about the bells. It was almost beyond belief when someone from out of town came up to me and said, "I was told to tell you that those bells are for a prophet in his own town." The next day, someone who had attended the St. Theresa's concert called the local newspaper and the following article was published two weeks later:

**"Tolling of Bells Seen as
Miracle by Parishioners"**

**By William Simbro
Des Moines Register Religious Writer
July 28, 1990**

The unexpected ringing of bells at a Des Moines church has become part of the mystery surrounding reported appearances of the Virgin Mary since 1981 that have drawn millions of pilgrims to the mountain village of Medjugorje, Yugoslavia.

At two dramatic moments in a program on Medjugorje at St. Theresa's Catholic Church, 1230 Merle Hay Road, the sound of church bells broke in. It brought surprise to some, thoughts of a miracle to others and tears to many. After most of the crowd of 400 had left, a small group who stayed to pray heard a third unexplained tolling of the bells.

The later discovery of a mechanical malfunction explained why bells rang but raised other questions.

Jerry Morin returned to his home parish July 15 to present his program. It was the church where he first felt a yearning to go to Yugoslavia to see the six young "visionaries" and experience Mary's reported messages to the world and such phenomena as healings, a "dancing" sun and Rosaries changing colors.

The Des Moines commercial real estate broker and former professional musician has recorded an album of songs about Medjugorje that he says God gave him, with a second album soon to be released. He gives his program around the country and has appeared at several conferences on Medjugorje.

Morin said he was shocked when the tolling began as he began quoting a reported message from Mary that "You are entering my times." He said it sounded like the bells of St. James Church in Medjugorje. At the intermission, several St. Theresa's members told him they didn't sound like the church's bells.

The church has a system programmed to play tapes of chimes through a belfry speaker five minutes before the 8, 9:30, and 11 a.m. Sunday Masses. The Westminster chimes are played at noon and 6 p.m. daily.

James Klemm, an electronic design engineer who looks after the equipment, was not at the event. He and a reporter this week went to the church to seek a logical explanation.

Klemm found that a program disk had, at an unknown time, failed to click over from a.m. to p.m., causing the chimes to play 12 hours later than intended, which corresponded to the times the bells were heard that night. "I find that really weird," said Klemm. "I wonder how long it has been this way and why no one had complained." Klemm clicked the disk to the proper setting.

Mysteries remain.

The bells sounded at emotional high points of the program. The crowd inside the church was able to hear the bells clearly, but a reporter later had to open a door to hear the outside speakers. There is a switch for playing inside, but several who were there said the sound came from outside.

Members also said the sound that night was not like that of St. Theresa's taped chimes.

"I've gotten to the point with this Medjugorje thing that I believe anything can happen," said Joseph Cortese, a Des Moines attorney and St. Theresa's member.

Said the Rev. Michael Peters, associate pastor at St. Theresa's, "People can speculate and make of it what they wish. A miracle takes place here every day. A piece of bread becomes the body of Christ. That's the miracle I see every day."

(Copyright 1990, reprinted with permission by

After the St. Theresa's presentation, I felt totally rejuvenated. All doubt and weariness had left me. I was bouyed by the awe that seemed to permeate every soul present. (Many people, even after seven years have passed, remember that night and still talk about the bells at St. Theresa's.) For me this was another great grace from God. This was the church where I "accidentally" met Regina. It was also named for the saint whose healing statue of Our Lady I had seen during "Lovely Lovely Lady". This was a wonderful church to have been given the gift of the bells and I thanked St. Therese for what I believed was her intercession.

The concert performed on that July evening proved to be the fuel and grace granted to us to be used for the weeks to come as we wrapped up the second collection of songs and continued the busy concert schedule.

God was helping me to understand one thing after another. Sometimes understanding would be revealed in song. Sometimes through the voice of Jesus, or even the voice of the Father as in "The Servant". The Holy Trinity was working. It became more evident to me that the Father, Son and Holy Spirit were concerned with the direction for our lives and most importantly our souls, as in this message from Our Lady in Medjugorje: *I want you to be happy here on earth and then to be with me later in paradise.*

My heart filled with appreciation for this loving and caring mother, always pleading, always wanting our choices to be right. I saw her simply as the reflection of an all-powerful, caring and loving God.

Another distinct change that was rapidly taking place in

me was a deepening of my understanding of the Holy Sacrifice of the Mass and a deeper appreciation for the Body, Blood, Soul and Divinity of Jesus truly present in the Holy Eucharist.

April 3, 1986: *Dear children! I wish to call you to a living of the Holy Mass...Jesus gives you His graces in the Mass. Therefore, consciously live the Holy Mass and let your coming to it be a joyful one. Come to it with love and make the Mass your own. Thank you for having responded to my call.*

The Blessed Virgin at Medjugorje

One of the greatest gifts within me was a deepening awareness of Satan and his cunning work to destroy lives, especially through greed, lust and the material allurements of life. I looked around at families and relationships literally being torn apart by him. It was comforting to know that Our Lady was here to help restore individuals and families by pointing them toward her Son. She seemed tireless in her desire to help restore goodness in our lives.

July 25, 1988: *Dear children, today I am calling you to a complete surrender to God...I am with you, even if you think Satan is in control. I am bringing peace to you...Thank you for having responded to my call.*

The Blessed Virgin Mary at Medjugorje

During this time I sensed that by saying "yes" to God I was joining all the saints who had gone before me. I realized I could draw on their help to fight the fight. This is also when I began to feel touched by angels in my apostolate.

It seemed for about a six-month period, everywhere I went people were seeing angels. One even identified my guardian angel as "George". I recall several concerts, all in different areas of the country, in which people were seeing these angels. The Angel of Defense was described as very large, about seven feet tall with full armor. His shield was always in front of me. Many confirmed this angel to be St. Michael the Archangel. The Angel of Zeal was seen at my side and was also very tall. A third angel was identified as the Angel of Truth. I was told that these three angels accompanied me wherever I went. At first, I passed it off as being hallucinatory, but the occurrences of angels seen by witnesses were so frequent and coincidental that I had to seriously consider that these angels were with me in this mission.

I had always known that celestial beings were all around us and I believed in a guardian angel all my own. However, it wasn't until time and again someone in the audience mentioned they had seen angels around me that I really began to appreciate the help they offer to all of us. Little did I know that I was about to need intercession from every heavenly entity.

Grace

Like conversion, justification has two aspects. Moved by grace, man turns toward God and away from sin, and so accepts forgiveness from on high.

Grace is the help God gives us to respond to our vocation of becoming his adopted sons. It introduces us to the Trinitarian life.

Sanctifying grace is the gratuitous gift of his life that God makes to us; it is infused by the Holy Spirit into the soul to heal it of sin and to sanctify it.

CHAPTER 14

Of the two conversions that are in the church; there are water and tears: the water of Baptism and the tears of repentance.

St. Ambrose

A SISTER'S CONVERSION

In October of 1991, I was invited to Great Falls, Montana, for some concert presentations. After one of the concerts, I called my mother just to say hello from the other side of the country. How terribly sad she sounded. She said that Claudette was very ill. The doctors had just discovered cancer in my sister and it was terminal. My heart sank to the floor. I told my mother I would be home as soon as possible.

The next week I was on my way to Massachusetts. The concern was evident on the faces of my brother and mother. Some years before, my sister in law, Bev, had beaten the odds with breast cancer. She was the only survivor from her support group. Would my family beat the odds one more time with this insidious enemy?

Claudette lived near my mother and brother, so in moments I was at her door. Upon entering her home I hugged her immediately and told her I loved her. She cried in my arms. She was afraid. My sister always seemed to be the pillar of strength, the one from whom we all drew courage. She was the joker, the life of the party. She always kept the family hopping by planning trips or events for everyone to do together. Her philosophy was to squeeze every ounce out of life. To the family, she was bigger than life and now she was weeping in my arms. I comforted her the best I could.

In her physical weakness, Claudette's faith was very great. She had the attitude and belief that God would heal her. She believed so strongly she would be healed, that she had me believing it would happen as well. However, she also knew the chances were very slim. She was a victim of ovarian cancer, a ravaging cancer that was consuming her body in a slow death. Conversely, she was willing to accept that if God's will was to take her, then let God's will be done.

For many months I traveled regularly to Massachusetts to be with my sister. We were extremely close and the thought of losing her ate at my heart. Every time I returned home to visit her, we would talk about Medjugorje and the messages of Our Lady. She always wanted to hear what Our Lady had to say, particularly about heaven, hell and purgatory. We would talk for hours about Our Lady's messages and matters of faith. I never would have believed that when writing "At The Cross", I would now be the one at the foot of the cross seeing my sister suffer.

I watched as Claudette walked step by step to conversion. At one time she said to me, "Why did it take this to happen to me to understand that God is all that matters?" She saw so clearly that all the material things are "just stuff." She acknowledged that only a year before, she and her husband were miraculously saved from a ravaging fire in their home. She said that if she had died in that fire, she wasn't sure she would have been heaven-bound. She said she had been given time for long-overdue confession and to pray. She really enjoyed praying and reading spiritual materials. She would have prayer vigils in her home with many friends and relatives gathering to pray the Rosary.

During Claudette's struggle, Regina and I had discerned that God wanted us to be more than friends. His guiding hand led us to a private marriage ceremony on the feast day of The Solemnity of Mary, January 1, 1992. We were married in Mary Immaculate Catholic Church in Kirksville, Missouri, and were both so thankful to God and Our Lady for this miracle of our sacrament.

Three months later Claudette called me and said they had stabilized the cancer. It seemed to be in remission. She said she felt prompted to come to the Heartland of America Marian Conference we were sponsoring in Des Moines in May, 1992.

Finally, the weekend of May 2nd arrived. My body was exhausted, yet my spirit was exhilarated. I was barely able to catch my breath as I made sure everything and everyone was in place. The image of the Blessed Virgin Mary was being projected on two large video screens for everyone's viewing and the song "The Lady of Medgugorje" was filling the auditorium. As so often seemed to be the case, my eyes welled with tears. This was the Heartland of America Marian Conference in Des Moines, Iowa. It had been months in the planning stage and I was functioning on my reserve tank of Holy Spirit energy. I was here in the midst of what appeared to be another wonderful miracle of grace.

With a contact set of headphones I was in communication with literally an army of volunteers, also tired from the many hours of sacrifice and preparation. As I scanned the large auditorium, my senses were filled with the sights and sounds of the more than nine thousand participants. A wonderful fragrance emanated from the superbly decorated main altar. Visually, a colorful splendor of numerous cut flowers and floral arrangements completely enclosed the stage area and main altar. Gracing the stage were beautiful, life sized, statues of Jesus and Mary, brought to us by friends in Kansas City, Missouri.

In my heart, I knew God had performed a miracle here in transforming this secular auditorium into a place of holiness that would serve to glorify God and bring great honor to the Blessed Virgin Mary. I glanced over to the side of the auditorium from my director's position and saw an unforgettable sight. Hundreds of people were waiting in lines to enter the Sacrament of Reconciliation. (I would later hear comments from many exhausted priests of their involvement for as long as fifteen hours of hearing confessions.)

My mind was photographing images that I knew would remain with me forever. I had been a guest presenter at numerous Marian conferences, but this one was different. As I studied each section of the auditorium, I recognized face after face. This was more than just an event I had helped organize; this was a family. It was then the realization came, that the hundreds of church concert presentations I had performed throughout Iowa and across the country for the past three years had planted numerous seeds of Catholic unity. Here we all were, under one roof to praise God and be recipients of His mighty works.

My heart was filled to the brim as I looked out over the crowd and saw my mother, my sister, Claudette, and my niece, Kerry. They had just flown in from Boston that morning. And now, here they were sitting in this giant auditorium that had been transformed into a house for God. I could compare the transformation in the auditorium to my sister's recent life. This person who had been so worldly was now overflowing with spirituality and grace. I looked down at my feet at the beautiful three-foot statue of Our Lady of Fatima I had just purchased for her. Claudette was going to love this! I could see her face from my director's vantage point. Claudette was still scared but we would all continue to pray for a miracle. It crossed my mind that if ultimately we could not save her body, then maybe this labor of love could contribute to saving her soul. Now I could bring this conference to a close knowing it so dramatically affected those I loved most.

Claudette remarked later that she never experienced anything so powerful as the conference. It completely changed her spiritual life. She said she could now truly accept whatever God's will was for her. Every minute of the conference with her daughter, Kerry, and our mother was a special grace.

I was so happy my mother could be present to witness another miracle of grace. Earlier, she conveyed to me that she, Claudette, and Kerry had all witnessed the "miracle of the sun" on their final approach to the Des Moines airport. I had no reason to doubt my mother, for she and I had seen this together before. (Later, during the conference, over five hundred people would witness this same phenomenon outside the auditorium. This imparted some assurance in my heart that we had done all we could in preparation for this event. I could only thank God and Our Lady for the opportunity to serve them in this fashion.)

My eyes then followed row by row along the many familiar faces until I reached the final row high up toward the rooftop. There, my eyes settled on the beautiful, full sized, painted silk banners hanging from the steel rafters. Like title-winning flags, eight of Our Lady's images hung majestically over the crowd, four on each side of the auditorium. The artist had captured, beyond any expectations, my vision of incorporating these banners into the event. Each silk panel depicted the image of a Catholic Church-sanctioned apparition site of the Blessed Virgin. In awe, I intently studied the 1858 apparition of Our Lady of Lourdes, France, when she revealed to young Bernadette Soubirous, "I am the Immaculate Conception." To the left was the apparition of Fatima, Portugal, where, in 1917, Mary appeared to three shepherd children as the Lady of the Rosary. Next was the depiction of Mary's sorrowful appearance to two young children at LaSallette, France. The final depiction on this side of the auditorium was a masterfully painted Lady of Mt. Carmel, when Mary, in 1251, in Aylesford, England, appeared to St. Simon Stock with the Rosary and the Scapular in hand. Turning to the opposite side of the auditorium, I continued to be awed by Mary's visits in Beauraing, Belgium, in 1932-1933 and in Banneux, Belgium, in 1933. Next was the banner depicting Mary's visit to Saint Catherine Laboure in the Rue du Bac of Paris, France, in 1830 where the "Miraculous Medal" was introduced. The final banner was the most recent Church-approved visit of Mary in Betania, Venezuela, in 1976. These works were an overwhelming sight and a tremendous addition to the conference.

My good friend and photographer, Bill, who I had twice taken to Medjugorje, was stationed at the video command center. He had spent many hours assisting me in meticulously guiding the successful implementation of the many technical aspects of this event. Regina's brother and sister-in-law, Jim and Kyle Clark and their music ministry "One Accord," were stationed on the second side stage ready to fill the auditorium with their glorious praise and worship music. At the far end of the auditorium many attendees were heading toward the chapel that had been created for adoration of the Blessed Sacrament.

Was this a glimpse of heaven? I could sense many hearts, minds and lives were being transformed during this event. In witnessing this miracle of grace I could not help but reflect on how my life arrived at this point. This did not happen overnight, nor was it solely a result of the many hours of preparation. More than three years before, I was faced with the decision of saying "yes" or "no" to a clear voice of instruction that I believe was the Holy Spirit. Somehow, through a mysterious sequence of instructions and "God-incidences," I was humbly brought to a point, whereby there could be no answer except "yes." That "yes" has translated itself into miracle after miracle of grace in my life.

As I looked again at the many people waiting in line for confession, the true purpose of this event was becoming evident. We had provided a medium in which the Holy Spirit could lead others to reconciliation, conversion of heart and a deeper, more meaningful understanding of our Catholic faith. I was fully aware of how God's mercy and grace can allow us all to be made new. I was thankful that my own footsteps to conversion years before could now be used to help others along their own path. I was especially thankful that I could be instrumental in my sister's footsteps toward conversion.

CHAPTER 15

If the greatest sinner on earth should repent at the moment of death, and draw his last breath in an act of love, neither the many graces he had abused, nor the many sins he had committed would stand in his way. Our Lord would receive him into His mercy.

St. Therese of Lisieux

A SISTER'S PROMISE

The following twelve months passed in a blur. Every one was praying for Claudette's healing. The year passed as though only a month. It seemed the *To The World* music was exemplified in her life and struggle to live. We had many talks about how the music affected her. One night when she was particularly suffering she called me in Des Moines to say she had just finished listening to the song "Live the Message" for the hundredth time. She said she believed God had me write the song just for her. She was sobbing on the phone.

In April of 1993, I was able to tell Claudette, almost miraculously for our ages, Regina and I were expecting a child. We planned to name the baby Mary Claudette-Therese if it was a girl. Claudette was so happy we were going to name the baby after her. She was very weak but was comforted by that thought. She had always told me she believed I was made for children. She knew the tragedies of my past, so this news was especially joyful to her.

Sadly, Claudette would never see my little girl. On May 25, 1993, my sister passed away. But, before she died, I made a promise to her. Due to having shared many of Our Lady's messages concerning souls in purgatory, I told her I would offer all of my concerts, daily Masses and Rosaries for her soul until I felt, or knew, she was in heaven, even if it meant the rest of my life. In return she promised me, "If there's any way I can let you know I'm in heaven, believe me I will." Later, I became especially conscious of the souls in purgatory who had no one to pray for them. I loved my sister so deeply. I knew I would keep my promise to her. It seemed to be something Claudette would want, so I also began to dedicate my Rosaries for the other souls in purgatory as well.

For over two years, I followed the almost daily routine of attending noon Mass and offering sacrifices and intentions for my sister. Our Lady had said that the souls in Purgatory could not pray for themselves, but our prayers were used to help them be purified and, subsequently, lead them to heaven. These words had new meaning for me now, as I prayed with a renewed vigor.

Time seemed to pass quickly. Time also seemed to have no immediate relevance, since there was no way I could know how long I would need to continue this supplication. Always in my mind were the words Claudette spoke to me three months before she died, "If there's any way I can let you know I'm in heaven, believe me I will." I believed her. When Claudette said she would do something, she had always done it. She had a sort of iron will when it came to accomplishing what she set her mind to do.

Many months had passed since her death. I quietly and soberly engaged in my efforts of keeping my promise to her. At times, I found myself very reserved and almost detached from everyone and everything in the world. I continued making concert and conference presentations, but the concern for Claudette was always in the forefront of my thoughts. The concerts and conferences were great opportunities to pray for Claudette and for my new family concerns. Although sometimes I would have to battle the doubts as to whether any of my prayers and sacrifices were being heard, I knew I would keep my promise. I could only hope that somewhere, somehow, Claudette and other souls were being affected and possibly being released from purgatory. I felt that I would never really know the answer until the end of my life. Even though the Blessed Mother clearly described heaven, hell and purgatory to many chosen visionaries, I knew that hardly anyone was ever given the privilege of knowing for sure the effects of their prayers for the souls in purgatory.

One of the messages of Our Lady I remembered reading was she had mentioned that if we could see the effects of our prayers we would want to pray all the time. The words from this statement alone had incredible implications regarding personal prayer. This statement of the Blessed Mother always stayed in my mind and it helped to diffuse the doubt about the effectiveness of my prayers.

One of the most exhilarating gifts I have ever received was to be at the birth of little Mary Claudette-Therese. My heart was immensely moved by my daughter's birth on December 29, 1993. Given my jaded past, to actually hold this little life in my hands was a joy beyond belief. To have lost one of my best friends in my sister and to experience this new life in my daughter were at times overwhelming and mystifying to me. I missed Claudette immensely. For over two years I followed as faithfully as possible the promise to her.

Regina and I were invited to sing and give witness at a weekend Marian conference when I first received a glimpse of the possibility of my prayers and sacrifices being answered. On Saturday night of the conference, Regina and I attended the conference speaker dinner. We sat on one side of a sizeable round dinner table. Seated opposite us at the table was one of the young Medjugorje visionaries. Everyone was enjoying the meal and conversation was plentiful amongst other invited guests at the table. It was at this point my thoughts wandered to my sister and I must have looked pensive. The English translator told me the young visionary wanted to know what was troubling me. Reluctantly, I explained I had been thinking about my deceased sister and the concern that I always carried with me. The translator asked what my sister's name was. After telling her "Claudette Richards" we continued with the meal and the subject was dismissed.

After a wonderfully Spirit-filled weekend, Regina and I returned to Des Moines. That night while having supper at home, we discussed the conversation that had taken place at the dinner table during the conference. Regina said what she always says best, "If God wants you to know about Claudette, then somehow that will happen. If He doesn't want you to know then just go on and continue what you are doing for her." We talked about it only a couple of times after that.

Approximately a year after that particular conference I was still in my routine of offering daily Mass, receiving the Holy Eucharist, praying my Rosary and offering concerts for Claudette. Regina and I were invited to present at another Marian conference. As we walked into the hotel lobby I noticed the same young visionary and same translator we had seen eleven months earlier. We had just begun to exchange greetings when the translator put her hands up to her mouth as if in amazement and concern. She immediately rushed over to me and wrapped her arms around my neck. She kept apologizing over and over, "I am so sorry Jerry. I tried calling you but I got no answer. I was supposed to tell you that the Blessed Mother conveyed that Claudette is in heaven!" Stunned, I asked, "Why did God want me to know this now?" The translator emphatically said for me to pray and God would let me know why. Slowly absorbing this incredible news, Regina and I went on to our room.

We closed the door of the hotel room and just stared at each other stunned and amazed. Then Regina whispered, "I think Claudette just found a way to let you know where she is." The emotions I was experiencing were beyond belief. Part of me believed this was true, while another part of me doubted because it was so unbelievable. I called my mother in Fitchburg, Massachusetts, and explained to her this news. She didn't know how to respond, but I could sense relief in her voice as if she immediately believed what I was telling her.

I hung up the phone and prepared to go to Mass. On the way to the conference hall, I heard the following words infused into my mind. "I HAVE WAITED FOR NOW TO REVEAL THIS TO YOU, FOR ANY OTHER TIME YOU WOULD HAVE DOUBTED TOO STRONGLY AND DISMISSED IT AS UNTRUE. I HAVE CHOSEN THIS TIME BECAUSE OF THIS DAY. THIS DAY WILL SERVE TO CONFIRM THAT THIS IS TRUE." I thought, "Because of this day? What does that mean?" I then asked, "What is today?

148

Is there any relevance to this day?" The driver of the van said, "This is All Saints Day. Tomorrow is All Souls Day." In the rush of going to that conference, I had forgotten what I had awakened that morning remembering. I felt those in the van would understand, so I shared with them what had happened. They were speechless. At once we all remarked we had the chills.

At the evening Mass, I was in awe and once again trying to assimilate the meaning of it all. I was unable to hold in the emotions running through me. I literally cried throughout the entire Mass. I realized, however, that unlike many of the tears in the past, these were tears of joy. Claudette was in heaven! It seemed a tremendous weight was lifted off of me. I sensed this was another healing bestowed upon me.

The concert presentation we performed the next day, All Souls Day, was one of the most freeing, powerful, and liberating presentations we had ever given. Just before making the presentation, another confirmation was given to me. We had been invited to this conference in large part to sing the conference theme song, "Live the Message." I was so honored to be a part of this wonderful conference. Just as I stepped onto the stage I realized I was about to sing the very song Claudette believed I wrote just for her. Here I was singing that song at a conference with the theme *Live the Message*. Was God trying to show me that this special message from Our Lady was, indeed, the truth? The sensation was overwhelming as I was singing. I sensed Claudette standing right next to me. Now I could rest in the belief that Claudette would be interceding, praying and helping me in my mission. I will always be eternally grateful for this intercessory act and this special grace from God and Our Lady.

CHAPTER 16

Few souls understand what God would accomplish in them if they were to abandon themselves unreservedly to Him and if they were to allow His grace to mold them accordingly.

St. Ignatius Loyola

THE JOURNEY CONTINUES

In June, 1997, a professional opportunity for Regina allowed me to resign from my job in Des Moines, Iowa, and concentrate on Respond Ministry. On my last day of employment I walked to the parking lot, as I had nearly every day for eight years. Once in my car I immediately received the lyrics to "Let Them Know The Reason". I pulled paper out of my brief case and quickly wrote the song as I sat in the parking lot. I had received continual promptings to write this narrative. It wasn't until this song was written that I knew the time was now.

LET THEM KNOW THE REASON
(To The World III)

Many need My love today, many need to know
The road that they may find their way back home
Distractions of the world you see
The seeds we need to sow
Let the music help to lead them safely to the fold

When you look into their eyes
Let My light shine through
Sing the Love I placed within your heart
Sing the words and melody as I give to you
Trusting that My love will see you through

Chorus
Let them know the reason for the songs you sing
Let them see the love deep in your heart
And when you look into their eyes,
Let My love shine through
It's My love from where your music starts

Let them know the reason you sing in this light
Let them know the reason the flame of love burns bright

And one more thing that should know
And this the very truth
Tell them it's I AM who sings in you

Instrumental

Distractions of the world you see
Seeds we need to sow
Let the music help to lead them safely to the fold

Then when you look into their eyes

151

Let my light shine through
Sing the love I've placed deep in your heart
Sing the words and melody as I give to you
Trusting that My love will see you through

Let them know the reason for the songs you sing
sing the love I've placed deep in your heart
And when you look into their eyes
Then I'll say through you
Pray that I may come and dwell in you

Several additional songs provided confirmation for not only this book, but for the *To The World III* collection. The following words were received during Holy Week in 1997. The time in which these words were received was again rapturous and mystifying. I quickly realized that what I was hearing was representative of the voices of both Jesus and Mary. These words still mystify me. I believe the relevance of this song is yet to unfold.

TWO HEARTS INSEPARABLE
(To The World III)

(Refrain)
We are two hearts inseparable
For those who have ears let them hear
These are the words that we give to you
Sing them, bring everyone near
We are two hearts inseparable

Harken to every word
I, your Mother Immaculate, and
I, your Jesus, your Lord

Please take courage my children
Listen for us and behold
Know that the secrets of heaven
Soon are about to unfold

For those who have ears let them hear
The trumpets are ready to blow
Be watchful with patient endurance
Dear children we love you so

Deep in the silence you'll hear us
Here you will know when we say
All for His plan of salvation
For it will be known from this day

We are two hearts inseparable...

In another rapturous moment the following words were
received. This song again characterizes the seriousness of
the mission I believe has been set before me, to set captives
free.

PROCLAIM MY NAME
(To The World III)

So you're deep in troubled waters
And you're starting to despair

You cannot see the answers
Yet you know they're there somewhere
And like a child you trust Him
And to Him you cast your fears
Then your faith starts rising, fears subsiding
Comes His voice to hear

Proclaim My Name! set the captives free
Proclaim My Name! for all the world to see
For it's by your own example of surrendering to Me
In My name will come all victory

It's not yourself you're fighting but in reality
The battle that is raging are principalities
Of yourself you have no power
But I grant the strength to win
Then My words your finding, light is shining
Then you hear again

Proclaim My name! Set the captives free
Proclaim My name! For all the world to see
For its by your own example of surrendering to me
In My name will come all victory

Proclaim My name! Set the captives free
Proclaim my name then truly free you'll be
Then when all is done and pass away
My words will still remain
Then you'll proclaim my name eternally

In following this journey, I wish to point out that songs written in my early conversion were gifts granted to me to express my relationship with God and love for Him. However, many of the songs written in recent years - "The Servant", "At The Cross", "Let Them Know the Reason", "Two

154

Hearts Inseparable" and "Proclaim My Name" are more direct and encompassing. There seems to be a fine line betweeen writing lyrics or music as a result of an inspiration and writing what appears to be a direct communication from heaven. These are two distinct and independent processes. I find the Holy Spirit can present an inspiration and words follow as a result of the inspiration. Generally, this process is preceded by a given experience or desire which leads to the expression of the experience in an inspired way. The other is more of a directive to write what is being given at that moment. An early example of this was when I received "Come To Me". These are two completely independent happenings. The fine line is the ability to recognize the difference between my desire and conscious effort to write an inspired song versus something I am being directed to wirite. In the latter, it is not my desire to write it nor is it received out of any particular inspiration. At these times it is instantaneous and encompassing and can happen at any moment without rhyme or reason. I write as it is being delivered to me. If I were to speak it as it is being delivered, I would be in awe at what I was hearing. The mysticism surrounding these moments humbles me to micro-smallness in proportion to its origin. In essence, the result is the knowledge that I am only a vessel used for the purpose of writing.

I believe that God's voice, as Father, Son and Holy Spirit, is accessible to all. His wisdom, understanding, knowledge, holiness and joy is for everyone. What does it take to receive this grace, the grace to hear? As I look back at these last eight years' experiences, I believe prerequisites are a desire to be right with God and a awareness that God is all that matters. Being in the posture of asking, seeking and knocking will lead to the beginning stages of healing, direction and purpose. A personal relationship with all three persons of the Blessed Trinity is for everyone. It is a free gift and no one has a monopoly on it. Jesus says, *You do not receive because you do not ask.*

If you, then, who are wicked, know how to give good gifts to your children, how much more will the Father in heaven give the Holy Spirit to those who ask him? (Luke. 11. 13)

God is waiting to communicate intimately with each person. When He does communicate, I believe it will be in a way that you will know unquestionably that it is God.

God always provides the grace if we truly and sincerely desire to change our ways. God knows the human heart. He knows every hair on our heads and He wants only what is good for us. Are we willing to make the necessary changes? Are we willing to surrender? Our Lady mentions the word surrender many times in her messages.

On completion of the final chapter of this book another unexpected grace occurred. God once again revealed His mercy. I had just completed reading the finished manuscript and had prayed the Rosary. Upon completion of the Rosary I was asking God's continued healing direction and purpose when I received the following:

FORGIVE ME FOR MY PART
(To The World III)

I'm sitting here and thinking about you
Wondering just how old you'ld be
Maybe blue eyes, maybe dark hair
I'm sorry for this tragedy

How could I think we were more important
What you'd be today I'll never know
Why did I believe we wouldn't love you
I want you now to know I love you so

Chorus

Part of me was lost for many years
And now that I have given you your names
I ask from my heart forgive me for my part
Mark and John I love you just the same
(Yes my sons I love you just the same).

This I'll need to sing out to the world now
There are many hurting can't you see
I pray that others also ask forgiveness
That the way the Master's healed me

It's coming 'round again to being my time
It's true now I know a father's love
Though my pretty girls are earthly angels
How will I tell them of my two above

Every time I hear them say I love you
And late at night they climb up on my knee
Then I know the joy that I've been given
I'm such a lucky man and now I see that…

Chorus

This I know is what I have to write now
I've thought about it from the very start
Now I know I'll have to sing about you
This great big world will know you're in my heart

Chorus

This conversion story began prior to any awareness of Medjugorje, but, for reasons that will always be a mystery, took its fulfillment in Medjugorje. In its fulfillment, it becomes truth that I serve as fruit of this ongoing event. I thank God for this special time of grace, healing and conversion. I find this conversion to be a day-to-day process, daily asking God to come into my life. It also means constantly surrendering fears, wants and desires and to trust in His divine will for my life. This is where lasting healing, direction, purpose and inner joy leading to peace come from.

Our Lady's messages have been planted in the soil of my heart, but like a seed that falls on fertile soil, the messages need constant nourishment in order to grow and bloom. That nourishment comes in living these messages of prayer, fasting, sacrifice, conversion, and peace. It's a daily, indeed sometimes hourly, challenge. As children of God and of Mary we need to strive to be the kind of seed that produces the fruit of being adequately nourished, and not the kind of seed that falls into the thorns, where the cares of this world choke out all nourishment. Our Lady's messages are life and nourishment because they mirror the Gospel messages of Jesus.

As I travel and present this witness and music I am constantly reminded of certain things. One is the third secret of Our Lady of Fatima that was never revealed by the Church. Our Lady instructed through Sister Lucia that the third secret was to be opened by the Holy Pontiff in 1960. Another thing I am constantly reminded of is a letter from Father Tomislav Vlassic to the Pope in 1983 in which he reports on the revelations which Mirjana (one of the visionaries of Medjugorje) received in 1982 and entrusted to him on November 5, 1983: Here are excerpts from that letter.

"After the apparitions of the Blessed Virgin on November 30, 1983, Maria Pavlovic (another of the visionaries) came to me and said, "The Madonna says that the supreme Pontiff and the Bishop must be advised immediately of the urgency and great importance of the message of Medjugorje.

This letter seeks to fulfill that duty.

Five young people (Vicka Ivankovic, Maria Pavlovic, Ivanka Ivankovic, Ivan Dragicevic, and Jakov Colo) see an apparition of the Blessed Virgin every day. The experience in which they see her is a fact that can be checked by direct observation. It has been filmed. During the apparitions, the youngsters do not react to light, they do not hear sounds, they do not react if someone touches them, they feel that they are beyond time and space.

All of the youngsters basically agree that:
"We see the Blessed Virgin just as we see anyone else. We pray with her, we speak to her, and we can touch her. The Blessed Virgin says that the world peace is at a critical stage. She repeatedly calls for reconciliation and conversion. She has promised to leave a visible sign for all humanity at the site of the apparitions of Medjugorje. The period preceding this visible sign is a time of grace for conversion and deepening the faith." The Blessed Virgin has promised to disclose ten secrets to us. So far, Vicka Ivankovic has received eight. Marija Pavlovic received the ninth one on December 8, 1983. Jakov Colo, Ivan Dragicevic and

Ivanka Ivankovic have each received nine. Only Mirjana Dragicevic has received all ten. These apparitions are the last apparitions of the Blessed Virgin on earth. That is why they are lasting so long and occurring so frequently.

...According to Mirjana, the Madonna confided the tenth and last secret to her during the apparition on December 25, 1982. She also disclosed the dates on which the different secrets will come to pass...

Mirjana said that before the visible sign is given to humanity, there will be three warnings to the world. The warnings will be in the form of events on earth. Mirjana will be a witness to them. Three days before one of the admonitions, Mirjana will notify a priest of her choice. The Witness of Mirjana will be a confirmation of the apparitions and a stimulus for the conversion of the world. After the admonitions, the visible sign will appear on the site of the apparitions in Medjugorje for all the world to see. The sign will be given as a testimony to the apparitions and in order to call the people back to the faith. That is why the Blessed Virgin continues to encourage prayer and fasting:

You have forgotten that through prayer and fasting you can avert war and suspend the laws of nature. After the first admonition, the others will follow in a rather short time. Thus people will have some time for conversion. That interval will be a period of grace and conversion. After the visible sign appears, those who are still alive will have little time for conversion. For that reason, the

Blessed Virgin invites us to urgent conversion and reconciliation. The invitation to prayer and penance is meant to avert evil and war, but most of all to save souls. According to Mirjana, the events predicted by the Blessed Virgin are near..."

Then the Blessed Virgin gave her the following message in substance:

"Excuse me for this, but you must realize that Satan exists. One day he appeared before the throne of God and asked permission to submit the Church to a period of trial. God gave him permission to try the church for one century. This century is under the power of the devil; but when the secrets confided to you come to pass, his power will be destroyed. For even now he is beginning to lose his power and has become aggressive. He is destroying marriages, creating divisions among priests and is responsible for obsessions and murder. You must protect yourselves against these things through fasting and prayer, especially community prayer. Carry blessed objects with you. Put them in your house, and restore the use of holy water."

.... After drafting this letter, I gave it to the youngsters so that they might ask the Blessed Virgin whether its contents are accurate. Ivan Dragicevic relayed the following answer: 'Yes, the contents of the letter are the truth. You must notify first the Supreme Pontiff and then the Bishop.

This letter is accompanied by fasting and prayers that the Holy Spirit will guide your mind and your

heart during this important moment in history.

Yours, in the Sacred Hearts of Jesus and Mary,
Father Tomislav Vlasic
Medjugorje, December 2, 1983.

In association with this letter, I had an unexpected visit with Father Petar Ljubjcic of the parish of Medjugorje. Father Ljubjcic is the priest chosen by the visionaries of Medjugorje to reveal the secrets to the world. He is author of <u>The Call of the Queen of Peace.</u> Father consented to answering my only two questions.

With the help of his translator Father responded to these questions. **"Do you really believe in your heart, Father, that you will see the day when you reveal the secrets to the world in advance of the events associated with them?** "Not only does Father believe that he will be revealing the secrets, but he believes he will be revealing them soon."

My second question; **"Father, if the days come when you do reveal the secrets, do you think they will have enough impact to change people's hearts back to faith?"** "Father believes it will be like today, where there are great natural disasters that are important one day and then forgotten the next. He believes that peoples' hearts are too concerned about the material things of this world and are growing increasingly cold. He believes that as these events occur and become more severe, they will not be able to be ignored. But by then it could be too late for many. Father constantly prays that peoples' hearts become receptive to Our Lady's messages."

In similar appearances in many of the approved apparitions throughout church history, Mary wants us to understand the importance of the times. These are sobering messages. However, we need not think in terms of gloom and doom. Even if God's appointed time for these events is soon, as Christians and as Catholics we must always have our attention on life eternal. Our Lady makes this clear in her messages that our lives are like a flower where we bloom for a short time and then fade. Our Lady wants us to be happy here and then with her in paradise afterward. This is the supreme reward of our faith, life eternal in heaven. Jesus said, *Amen, I say to you, unless you turn and become like children, you will not enter the kingdom of heaven.* Therein lies the secret of faith.

I wish to share one more event that is always with me. In the Catholic Church-approved apparition of 1846 at La Salette, France, Our Lady, after revealing much regarding the last days of the end times to the young French shepherdess, Melanie Calvat, said the following regarding a future time:

I call on the true disciples of the living God, who reigns in heaven; I call on the true followers of Christ made man, the only true Savior of men; I call on my children, the true faithful, those who have given themselves to me so that I may lead them to my Divine Son, those whom I carry in my arms, so to speak, those who have lived according to my spirit. Finally I call upon the Apostles of the Last Days, the faithful disciples of Jesus Christ...It is time they come out and filled the world with light. Go and reveal yourselves as my cherished children. I am at your side and within you, provided that your faith is the light which shines upon you in these unhappy days. May your zeal make you hunger for the glory and the honor of Jesus Christ. Fight, children of light, you, the few who can see. For now is the time of all times....

The Blessed Virgin Mary at La Salette

Remember how in Holy Scripture (Jonah. 3:10), Jonah was directed by God to convey the message of the impending destruction of the sin-laden city of Nineveh? Immediately, the Ninevites began intense prayer and fasting. When God saw what they did and how they turned from their evil ways, He had compassion and did not bring upon them the destruction He had threatened.

Similarly, Mary pleads for all her children to be reconciled, purified and made whole. In her messages conveyed in numerous apparitions throughout history, she urges everyone to turn from sin and assures us that God does respond to prayer and fasting. The Blessed Virgin Mary reminds the young visionaries of Medjugorje that these penitential acts can mitigate impending chastisements and even stop wars. Should we live in fear of what God holds for the future of this world? Rather, our energies should be spent on centering prayer around the hope that the world will respond to Our Blessed Lady's appeal for conversion, as the city of Nineveh did in response to Jonah's warning of old.

There are many wonderful books written on Medjugorje and most of the prior, approved places of Mary's visits from historical, analytical and theological perspectives. The purpose of this witness is to simply serve as one of many types of good fruit which bear forth from this powerful tree, Medjugorje, planted by God and Our Lady. The sinner has been forgiven and allowed to bloom.

I thank God every day that I have been given a second chance at life. It is a most humbling gift to be serving Him in this fashion. I am especially grateful for the wonderful partner and wife he brought to me in Regina Marie. And I thank Him for the two little gems granted to me through her, Mary Claudette-Therese and Andrea Marie and also for Regina's two sons Samuel and Nicholas. Family is one of God's greatest gifts.

Another blessing we attribute to God and Our Lady is the love that we share with countless people we have been privileged to know in this ministry. If the road to conversion leads to heaven, we don't want to go there alone. I think it will be marvelous to be doing concerts there. Can you even imagine the sounds, voices, orchestra and music? St. Francis of Assisi once wrote that he was visited by an angel who played only one note on the violin. That one note put him into ecstasy. I wonder if I'll have the chills there.

I seek only to follow the Holy Spirit's lead and to fulfill that which has been asked of me. As Father Svet exhorted me, "Keep singing, just keep singing."

I believe this book and its contents can be best summarized and characterized by the Scripture passage of Ephesians. 2: 4-8.

But God, who is rich in mercy, because of the great love he had for us, even when we were dead in our transgressions, brought us to life with Christ, raised us up with Him and seated us with Him in the heavens in Christ Jesus, that in the ages to come he might show the immeasurable riches of His grace in his kindness to us in Christ Jesus. For by grace you have been saved through faith, and it is not from you; it is a gift of God.

If this book or the *To The World* music draws only one person back to God, then the purpose for this work will have been fulfilled. Our eternal life is what counts, so we need to help bring as many as possible the message of how necessary it is to not make ludicrous decisions and to realize just how transitory are our lives and material possessions. What we do, or don't do here determines where we spend eternity. Helping others to start on their path toward conversion of heart and mind will make it all worth the effort. This journey toward heaven is a daily struggle for all of us and we need all the grace we can get.

May God grant you the courage and love to walk toward conversion and holiness. Let us pray from our hearts for one another so that we may stay ever so close to His throne room of grace and Our Lady's mantle of protection.

Even if the skies fill with fire and I am faced with the darkest of nights, I hope somehow, somewhere, you will hear me singing to the world "O the lady is calling, is calling us all...."

Come, Holy Spirit, Illuminator of the mind, heart and soul. We invoke You to bring forth Your light, making clear to all the purpose for which we are called. Bring us the assurance and peace of knowing that we belong to You, Spirit of the Triune God, and make us susceptible to Your promptings. Grant us the courage and love to act on Your behalf. Most Divine Advocate, Paraclete of Light, descend upon us now, making us mindful of Your most holy presence. Let Your gifts be manifested in and through us for the edification of Christ's Body, the Church. Amen. Come, Holy Spirit, come.

-Jerry Morin
April 12, 1989
On return from Medjugorje

EPILOGUE
by
Fr. Petar Ljubicic, O.F.M.

Respected & Dear Friends:

You have read this moving book *To The World - A Conversion Story* by the recognized Jerry Morin. You have surely once again come to realize that God is at work in Medjugorje and the power of His grace. It is hard to write down what a man feels when God begins to work in his heart and brings about salvation.

Jerry Morin, just like every man (pilgrim) was looking for peace of mind, true joy, and real happiness. He came to Medjugorje to the Queen of Peace and she as a mother accepted him. From the time he realized where he was, he opened himself completely to God. Something great happened, a miraculous and moving conversion. God has taken a hold on Jerry's life and Jerry cannot go on without God. He wants to live with and for God, and that is why he wrote about the experiences he had. He wants to be able to use these experiences to give God thanks and praise through the intercession of our mother in heaven, the Queen of Peace.

Conversion is truly an undeserving gift of grace. For Jerry, conversion is a grace-filled feeling that God is present, that He loves us, and that He wants us to have eternal happiness. He understood what Our Lady has constantly been repeating, that God must be first in our lives, more important than anything else. That means that our life only has real meaning when it is in accordance with God's plan for us. God's plan is for everyone that comes to know God, that loves Him with his whole body, that gives himself totally and joyfully worships and prays in order to become more perfect and holy. Man receives true joy and peace of mind and then he feels saved.

This time is truly a time of great grace and moving conversions, a time of ardent prayer and complete surrendering to God. The apparitions of Our Lady in Medjugorje, which have lasted for seventeen years, are proof of that. Some say that this act of God is so great that it is one of the most remarkable events of the past centuries, possibly the greatest happening since Pentecost!

The theme of Pentecost is still present in Christ's Church. Jerry's conversion is proof of that, and the millions of pilgrims that have come to Bijakovici, in the parish of Medjugorje, are witnesses to that. Who could count all of those who say that the days spent in Medjugorje were the happiest days of their lives? Many leave in tears when leaving that peaceful place saying they are leaving a part of themselves behind.

Many have said:
"In Medjugorje I found the peace that I was looking for all my life!"
"In that graceful place I learned how to pray with my heart!"
"While praying on Apparition Hill I felt God's closeness and His love."
"Since I was in Medjugorje I go to church every Sunday."
"While in Medjugorje I felt what the meaning of the Holy Mass was for the first time in my life and how much Jesus loves us!"
"I could never forgive, but since I had confession in Medjugorje, I received the grace to forgive easily."

We hear from all sides, how the "final days" are coming. Jesus

Himself spoke of the final happenings: *Many false prophets will arise and deceive many; and because of the increase of evil doing, the love of many will grow cold. But the one who perseveres to the end will be saved.* (Matt. 24, 11-13).

This history is coming to an end. Satan is hard at work. He uses all of his tricks, he confuses and brings unrest and uncertainty. He wishes to destroy all of God's plans. Our Lady has repeated this many times.

Cold love can be seen especially in hate and revenge, wars and the killing of the innocent, unborn children. Incurable diseases and the drug plague consume more and more people. Those are all signs that we have already fallen into the "final days" by Christ's and St. Paul's accounts. There is no more room for fear and despair. Faith and total surrender to God can beat anything.

It is interesting to read how St. Louis de Montfort in his writings professes that in the "final days" devotion to Our Lady will increase, that is, that the growth of Marian devotion is a sign of the "final days".

Our Lady's apparitions in Lourdes, Fatima, and Medjugorje have become a sign in "Mary's Centuries" and her great concern to help all people as a powerful intercessor. The last three years of this century are dedicated to Jesus Christ, the Holy Spirit, and God the Father. We need to use this time of grace for ourselves and for others.

Let us believe like Mary believed and let us love the way she did. Let us live every moment of our lives so that in prayer we will, like Mary, use the times for our salvation and for the salvation of others.

A mother asked her daughter upon her return from

Medjugorje, "My daughter, did you see Our Lady in Medjugorje?" A little surprised by the question the little girl didn't allow herself to get confused, but answered instead, "Mom, in Medjugorje there are Mount Krizevac, Apparition Hill, and a beautiful big church, and in this place with nothing, you can find everything. I was on Apparition Hill. I was praying. I will never forget this prayer. For the first time in my life I felt that God was listening to my prayer. I felt that He loves me and that He has a plan for me. That was my first experience with God. Mom, you know that I always prayed and went to holy Msass regularly. I felt that Jesus was my big brother. He became that because of His love for me and for all mankind. He was born, lived, suffered, carried His heavy cross on Calvary and died on it all for me. Is there greater love than that? I'm sure that there isn't. Why didn't I know that before? It was necessary for me to go to that graceful place for me to experience that. There on the mount, where the sky opened and where Our Lady, Queen of Peace, came to us. I felt that Our Lady was my mother and that she was appearing for me. My heart was constantly saying works of thanks, 'Thank you, mother, for these times! These times are graceful and saving! Everything is clear to me now. You, Our Lady, came here to take us to your son, Jesus. In Him we can have everything, joy and peace, love and happiness in life. Jesus, enter my heart and from this day I only wish to belong to You. I pray You give me the strength to give myself to You completely." This is how the little girl answered her mother's question on whether she saw Our Lady.

This moving meeting with Our Lady of Medjugorje became unforgettable for this young soul. These meetings change entire lives.

Our Lady came to Medjugorje and has been appearing this long so that she can help everyone. There have never been anywhere, or at anytime in the history of mankind, apparitions for this long and in this way. Six visionaries were fortunate enough to see the sky open and speak with our Heavenly Mother.

Our Lady is constantly asking us to convert. She wishes for our entire life to be a prayer and that we have strong faith in God, that is that we give ourselves to Him completely. Our Lady has stressed that renunciation and fasting is necessary for spiritual growth. Conversion, faith, prayer, and fasting arc not possible without forgiveness. That is why Our Lady wants us to go to confession regularly. Holy Mass is the height of our Christian life and believers live from that miracle.

Who accepts these calls to faith seriously and tries to live them will have peace, will be truly joyful and will really feel happy. That is exactly what the Queen of Peace wants with these apparitions. That is why this is the most important time of our lives. Let us use it the best that we can.

Fr. Petar Ljubicic is the Author of The Call of the Queen of Peace and is the priest chosen by the Medjugorje visionaries to announce to the world certain future events associated with Our Lady's visits.

respond ministry

Blessings and Graces
of
To The World

So by their fruits you will know them
(Matthew. 7: 20)

Over the years we have been humbled by the countless letters we have received from listeners of the *To The World* music. Following are just a few of their remarks. We will always be grateful for having received far more than we have given.

"The tape *To The World* is beautiful! It will continue to be a blessing. I am writing to say I am moved by its many pieces. The "Lady of Medjugorje" is a wonder! Thanks for being the instrument who brought it from the higher world!"

Minneapolis, Minnesota

"If just listening to these (CD's) brings such a powerful surge of emotion over me-I can't see how I can survive a concert, when I know the presence of Our Lady and the Holy Spirit would most definitely be even stronger."

Edmonton Alberta, Canada

172

"It would take pages to tell you what 'At the Cross' means to me."

New Albany, Indiana

"I feel so high- I'm not sure I'll ever come down, and I'm certain my life will never be the same."

Long Island, New York

"Because of the overwhelming feeling of God's grace that was there throughout the presentation, I knew instantly that going to this one event was a life-changing experience... Three of the greatest privileges of my life have been to be accepted into Diaconate formation and ordained ministry, to be involved in the 1992 Des Moines Marian Conference and to have the opportunity to work with our area-wide Marian prayer group these past seven years....None of this would have come about had it not been for Jerry Morin and Respond Ministry."

Des Moines, Iowa

"I heard your concert on the 21st day of July, and I couldn't help going back the next day. Never, never, never stop doing what you are doing; awakening us to the need to pray, pray, pray. I was so enlightened. Our Lady and the world needs you.

Louisville, Kentucky

"Thanks for saying yes to Our Lady. Your personification of her is done with real love. Know that you touch many hearts through your ministry."

Greeley, Colorado

"I went to see you a second time, the word that kept coming to me from seeing you was reconciliation....Two weeks later on the first Saturday of June I made my first confession in about 20 years...It's so purifying...I want

173

everyone to experience it!"

Albuquerque, New Mexico

"I don't know how to describe it but I was in a trance-like state for almost 3 days...I felt so happy yet all I wanted to do is play your tape, pray and cry. I felt like something broke open in me. I felt God's love so strong in my life.

Charlotte, North Carolina

"...and after three months I am still experiencing the tremendous grace poured out at the Marian conference in Des Moines.

Fargo, North Dakota

"Te amo y ta musica mucho! Gracias a Dios y el Spiritu Santo y La Neuestra Senora."

Etobicoke Ontario

"...the Heartland Of America Marian Conference was the most awesome display of Holy Spirit I have ever witnessed... I'm glad we were there."

Omaha, Nebraska

"Jerry's tapes are played daily by many people. They are finding peace in their hearts by listening to the beautiful music"

South Bend, Indiana

"Your presentation brought a true feeling of Mary's presence. I never specifically had felt Mary before. I Didn't just feel Mary, I felt her love. Closing my eyes, listening to the words of your songs and the words of her messages, I felt was if Mary was actually saying it all Herself. Thank your for that experience."

Portland, Oregon

"Your songs ignite a wound of love for God in my heart. They cause the glowing embers to blaze. Your songs in reality are prayers. When I hear you sing your 'prayers' tears of love and joy just seem to flow."

Pittsburgh, Pennsylvania

"This beautiful music brings me closer to God."

Liverpool, England.

"I was present at the St. Joseph, MO conference. I heard many speakers from all over the world. One speaker/ singer that really touched me was Jerry Morin. He sang an incredibly powerful song in his fight against abortion. Here are the words to "Say Yes"…(a letter to the editor)

Muscotah, Kansas

"I listen to your music played on KBVM (Blessed Virgin Mary) Radio all the time. It is like an actual grace to hear your music. Many times it brings me to tears."

Ft. Myers, Florida

"This shows evidence of what God is doing with Jerry and what God is doing for the church through beautiful music."

**-Mother Angelica
EWTN**

"Keep praying, keep listening, keep doing."

-Wayne Weible

"How I love *To The World*! It is exquisitely beautiful, just like the beautiful Mother who inspired Jerry. I know its healing will help bring Mary's peace to so many of God's hurting children."

-Rita Klaus

"One of the most powerful moments of closeness with Christ that I have recently experienced occurred when Jerry Morin sang "Say Yes" at the Mid America Marian Conference on the eve of Mary's Birthday, September 7th in St. Joseph, Missouri. Mostly everyone was moved to tears. I know I was. It was an anointed song at a crucial time in history...Sing it Jerry! 'Say yes.' Choose life!"

-Father Bill McCarthy
(My Father's House)

"I applaud you on your efforts to bring this message to the world and I congratulate you on the level of quality you have achieved in both your writing, your performance, and in the recorded quality."

-John Michael Talbot

"Keep singing. Just keep singing."

-Fr. Svetozar Kraljevic, O.F.M.
Parish of Medjugorje

"We stood in tears at the Notre Dame Medjugorje Conference listening to you sing "The lady is calling", then rushed to buy the cassette. We listened to it for the entire two hour trip back to Chicago. It became our favorite Marian hymn of all time - until we heard you and Regina sing 'At The Cross', which calls us to repentence every time we hear those hauntingly beautiful lyrics and music."

-Larry and Mary Sue Eck
Medjugorje Magazine

Bibliography

De Sola Chervin, Ronda. Quotable Saints. Servant
Publications, ©1992.

Butler's Lives of the Saints, Four Volumes, edited and revised and
supplemented by Herbert J. Thurston, S.J., and Donald
Attwater (Westminster, Maryland; Christian Classics,
1956).

Morin, Jerry. To The World - Live The Message; Respond Ministry,
Inc., 1989.

Excerpts from the English translation of the Catechism of the
Catholic Church for use in the United States of America
Copyright ©1994, United States Catholic Conference,
Inc.—Libreria Editrice Vaticana. Used with permission.

St Teresa of the Child Jesus. EDITIONS DE L'OFFICE CENTRAL,
51 RUE du Carmel, LISIEUX (Calvados) France. Printed
at the Printing Press of the Master Printer Draeger Broth
ers at Paris May 17, 1955.

The New American Bible. Catholic Book Publishing Co. New York.
Copyright ©1970 by the Confraternity of Christian
Doctrine, Washington D.C., including the revised New
Testament, Copyright ©1986.

All song lyrics from the *To The World I & II* music collections
Copyright ©1990, 1991 except, "Let Them Know The
Reason", Forgive Me For My Part", "Two Hearts
Inseparable", "Proclaim My Name" and "Come To Me"-
Copyright ©1998.

respond ministry

RESPOND MINISTRY MISSION

Formed in 1989, Respond Ministry, Inc. is a non-profit ministry with a purpose of acting as a catalyst through the intercession of Our Lady and the Holy Trinity in leading peoples' hearts and minds back to God.

We have been called to evangelize through the mediums of personal witness, concert presentations, Catholic conferences, original *To The World* musical collections and other *To The World* Respond Ministry products.

This apostolate has discerned it plays a role in Our Lady's great plan unfolding for the salvation of mankind. All income is through donations through the offering of its concert presentations and unique original products. One of our beneficiaries is the Retirement Fund for Religious in Washington, D.C.

Also, as a result of The Heartland of America Marian Conference in Des Moines, Iowa, in 1992, Respond Ministry sent $37,000 to Bosnia for food, equipment and relief efforts. Your contributions and all purchases through this ministry are considered donations and are tax deductible. We ask your help in becoming partners with us in this important on-going mission.

To schedule a *To The World* multi-media concert presentation you may contact Respond Ministry in the following ways:

RESPOND MINISTRY
P.O.BOX 7710
DES MOINES, IOWA 50322

Telephone and fax 1-800-835-8124
Telephone 573-499-0260
Additional fax 573-499-3891
Visit our new web site @

WWW.RESPONDMINISTRY.COM

Here you will be able to view and hear the different products offered by Respond Ministry and author/composer Jerry Morin. Also, this site will provide Our Lady's monthly message, on-going concert schedule, updates on upcoming Respond Ministry sponsored Catholic conferences, updates on *To The World III - Be Converted* recording project and other information.